Debits and Clearings Statistics

and Their Use

GEORGE GARVY

Adviser

Federal Reserve Bank of New York

Board of Governors
of the Federal Reserve System
Washington

First edition, first printing, January 1952

Second printing, June 1953

Third printing, December 1955

Revised Edition, May 1959

Library of Congress Catalog Card Number 59-60041

Foreword to the First Edition

Collection of debits statistics exemplifies the technical work of the Federal Reserve System in obtaining the factual basis of policy determination. Bank debits measure the extent to which depositors are using the funds in their accounts at commercial banks and, in conjunction with deposit figures, are a means of determining the rate of turnover of bank deposits, which are the chief component of the money supply. Information concerning the use of money is one of the essential requirements of effective monetary and credit policy.

Debits statistics have been widely used in public and private economic research ever since their initial publication by the Federal Reserve System in 1919. In combination with clearings statistics that extend, for New York City, back to the year 1853, debits have been one of the major economic series used by students of business cycles and by economic analysts. Nevertheless, no systematic study of the development and use of the debits series and their relationship to the longer run clearings series was available until Mr. Garvy undertook the project for his doctoral dissertation. In order that all users of the data may have a better understanding of their meaning, and hence of their appropriateness for different types of economic analysis, Mr. Garvy's major findings are presented in this study.

OLIVER S. POWELL, MEMBER
BOARD OF GOVERNORS OF THE FEDERAL RESERVE SYSTEM

Author's Preface

The first edition of this pamphlet was published in 1952 under the title *The Development of Bank Debits and Clearings and Their Use In Economic Analysis.* It was largely based on a doctoral dissertation submitted to Columbia University. In its preparation, the author received generous advice and many stimulating suggestions from Professor Arthur F. Burns. The original edition (now out of print, but which the interested reader can consult in leading university and public libraries) contained additional detail on New York City clearings and debits and an analysis of the relationship between clearings and debits in selected centers. The reader interested in this material is referred to the three appendixes included in the original edition, which also contains a more extended historical bibliography.

A revision of this pamphlet was necessitated by the revision of debits statistics which the Federal Reserve System undertook in 1953 and which incorporated most of the suggestions made in the concluding chapter of the original study. This revision required the rewriting of the concluding chapter and of the descriptive material on current debits and velocity statistics in Chapters III and VII. Less substantial revisions were made in the other chapters, and throughout an effort was made to bring statistical and analytical material up to date, usually through 1958. It was not feasible, however, to bring up to date the discussion on the use of measures of velocity in monetary theory and analysis without substantially expanding the pamphlet. A separate study on this subject is in preparation at the Federal Reserve Bank of New York.

The author owes a large debt of gratitude to numerous individuals, both in and outside the Federal Reserve System, for supplying factual information and statistical data. Several members of the research departments of the various Federal Reserve Banks and of the staff of the Board of Governors read the manuscript of the first edition and made valuable suggestions. The author wishes to acknowledge in particular the assistance of Clay J. Anderson, Economic

Adviser of the Federal Reserve Bank of Philadelphia, and Harold L. Cheadle, Senior Economist of the Federal Reserve Bank of Chicago, who served as members of a technical committee to review the study, and of John E. Horbett, then Assistant Director of the Board's Division of Bank Operations. Marie Butler's advice in organizing the cumbersome manuscript replete with technical details was invaluable. Alma M. Schumacher and M. H. Schwartz, formerly of the staff of the Federal Reserve Bank of New York, skillfully assisted the author in obtaining and organizing the statistical material and in many other ways. Robert C. Holland, Vice President of the Federal Reserve Bank of Chicago, reviewed the present revised edition and made numerous valuable suggestions. The author alone, however, is responsible for all interpretations and conclusions.

GEORGE GARVY

Contents

Tables

I. Introduction

Probably no monetary statistics released by the Board of Governors of the Federal Reserve System are more widely reproduced than debits statistics. Their extensive use, notwithstanding the considerable increase in the scope of monetary and banking statistics and the more adequate data on income and expenditures that have become available during the past two decades, is due to four principal reasons:

1. Debits are available very promptly, much earlier than such other comprehensive over-all estimates as the gross national product and also more promptly than any other important economic time series of national scope.

2. Debits are one of the few types of economic data that, being available for a large number of individual cities, can be used in analyzing local business developments.

3. Debits are used in computing the rate of turnover of deposits, an important tool of monetary analysis.

4. Comparable debits figures, together with their predecessor series, clearings, are available on a monthly and even weekly basis for a relatively long period of time. Hence they are an indispensable tool of business cycle research.

In this pamphlet an attempt is made to combine a study of the clearings and debits series—by necessity a highly technical matter—with a broad investigation of the contributions these series have made to economic analysis and of the services they have rendered to the economic analyst, historian, and theorist. The history of the two series is a necessary prerequisite to assessing their interpretive value and their relationships to various other economic measurements.

As with many economic time series whose usefulness is firmly established, there is less understanding than might be expected of the precise meaning and technical limitation of clearings and debits, respectively, and of the ways in which these two series differ in coverage and composition. The present study reviews the origin and

1

gradual improvement of both series and the difficulties inherent in their compilation and interpretation. The analysis is limited to the United States, although clearings, debits, or similar data on the volume of deposit money payments have been collected in a number of foreign countries.

Clearings and debits are the only statistical series covering a relatively long period that relate—even though only indirectly—to the monetary value of aggregate expenditure on final product. The volume of checks and drafts exchanged at local clearing house associations—commonly referred to as "clearings"—was one of the first types of accounting data obtained as a by-product of business operations to be used in economic analysis. In contrast to some important but more recent monetary series, such as total deposits of commercial banks, clearings were among the first current business statistics published regularly in this country. It was not until after World War I that bank debits, a newly developed series related to the volume of check payments, generally superseded the older series.

Bank clearings was one of the first historical series used to investigate the cyclical pattern of economic change in this country. The limited number of economic time series which reach relatively far into the past is not generally realized. Of the more than 800 monthly and quarterly United States economic time series collected (and in some cases compiled) by the National Bureau of Economic Research, only 89 reach back for more than 50 years.[1] The pioneers of quantitative economics, and in particular the early investigators in the field of economic fluctuations, had even fewer time series at their disposal. Among these, clearings occupied a particularly important place. Their continuity and their availability on a weekly and monthly basis made them especially attractive to students of economic fluctuations.

In most cases, continuous data on bank clearings are available from the time local clearing houses began operations. Thus, for New York City monthly clearings first became available in October 1853. Because of the general interest in clearings figures, which prior to World War I were almost the only time series reflecting general

---

[1] Arthur F. Burns and Wesley C. Mitchell, *Measuring Business Cycles*, Table 2.

business conditions available on a weekly basis, they were (and still are) transmitted telegraphically to New York and published in newspapers and various periodicals throughout the country. Several students of business cycles have made an effort to carry clearings data back as far as possible and to combine series for individual cities into comprehensive nationwide series.

The main weakness of the clearings data is their failure to include checks deposited for credit and chargeable against other accounts at the same bank, checks cashed over the counter, checks collected directly through the mails, and numerous types of charges to depositors' accounts in addition to those arising from the payment of checks. On the other hand, clearings are inflated by the inclusion of interbank payments, a large part of which duplicate other clearings transactions because they arise from bank collection of commercial checks. Also, the consistency over time of the clearings data is known to be considerably affected by bank mergers, changes in the membership of individual clearing houses, and changes in collection practices of commercial banks and in operating procedures of clearing house associations.

These and other shortcomings of the clearings data caused the Federal Reserve System to develop a more consistent and more representative series of deposit money payments. In August 1918, the Federal Reserve Banks began to collect weekly reports on "debits to individual accounts" on a uniform basis for a large number of cities in which clearing house associations were in operation.[2] The Board of Governors soon began to release national weekly and monthly series as well as separate figures for each reporting center.

Debits statistics have been revised several times since their inception, for the last time in 1953. This last revision followed most of the suggestions made in the first edition of this pamphlet. The debits series published currently covers debits to demand deposits, other than Government and interbank, at commercial banks holding practically all demand deposits in 344 reporting centers throughout the country, including almost all the large and medium-sized cities,

---

[2] It would probably have been equally easy to collect credits rather than debits to deposit accounts and the resulting series would have been of almost identical value for the purpose for which the debits series was intended.

and a sizable sample of smaller cities of around 20,000–30,000 population.

Most reported debits represent payments of checks drawn against demand deposit accounts, but some unknown proportion represents other charges which involve no checks. These include a customer's instruction to his bank (orally, by mail, or otherwise) to purchase securities or foreign exchange, or to perform some other transaction or service, and to charge his account.

For the years following World War I, bank debits have been used by statisticians and economists in preference to clearings figures because for analytical purposes they are clearly superior to the older series. Debits reflect the dollar value of current production and distribution to the extent that they cover deposit money payments for final products as well as for materials, wages and salaries, dividends, rents, and interest. But the inclusion of payments for identical goods at different stages of production and distribution results in many duplications, the degree of duplication varying among industries and over time. Debits, moreover, include payments for property and other financial transactions that do not necessarily arise from current production and distribution. Debits are therefore a broad measure of the use of deposit money for all purposes, including those which are only indirectly or not at all related to the level of gross national product.

As background for the discussion of the use of clearings and debits in monetary analysis and in business cycle research and forecasting, Chapters II and III respectively review the origin and development of clearings and debits statistics. Special attention is paid in these two chapters to the New York data and to the factors which make their level and fluctuations differ from those for the rest of the country. Chapter IV provides a comparative analysis of clearings and debits for the period for which both types of data are available. In Chapter V the relationship between clearings and debits and gross national product is investigated. The seasonal and cyclical behavior of clearings and debits is studied in Chapter VI. The following chapter deals with the measurement of deposit turnover derived from clearings and debits.

The use of clearings and debits in studies of business cycles is traced in Chapter VIII. Since clearings and debits, and measures of deposit velocity derived from them, featured prominently in the controversy centered around the validity of the quantity theory of money as reformulated by Kemmerer and Fisher, Chapter IX is devoted to the use of these empirical data in studies of monetary economics. In the final chapter, the main findings of the study are reviewed.

II. Clearings Statistics

Check clearings represent the volume of total check exchanges reported by individual clearing houses. There are more than 200 individual centers for which clearings data are available, in some cases for a considerable span of time. Unlike bank debits, clearings statistics are not collected and released by an official agency having a trained statistical staff. No statistical agency has ever collected or checked data released by all clearing houses in the United States, but some of the financial periodicals—notably the *Commercial and Financial Chronicle*—have exercised great care in securing and compiling clearings data. Obviously clearings data do not possess the same degree of uniformity and comprehensiveness that characterizes debits.

This chapter covers the entire period for which clearings statistics are available—since 1853 for New York City and since 1875 for a sufficiently representative group of cities throughout the rest of the country. Since 1919, however, analysts generally use the more comprehensive debits statistics in preference to clearings statistics in current economic analysis as well as in studies of cyclical fluctuations and long-run economic growth. While the discussion of clearings statistics is carried beyond 1918, this is done mainly to lay the groundwork for Chapter IV, in which clearings are compared with debits in order to evaluate the interpretive value of clearings for earlier decades for which they are about the only available statistical information on the size of money flows.

NATURE OF CLEARINGS STATISTICS

Clearings statistics are a natural by-product of daily collection activities of commercial banks throughout the country. "Clearings" represent the dollar volume of checks and drafts (and of some other cash items) exchanged daily by the members of a local clearing house association. While the details of clearing procedures are not the same in all cities, essentially identical basic operations are involved.

At an appointed hour, clerks of the participating banks appear at the clearing house with prepared bundles of checks ("exchanges") against all other participating institutions. The total amount "brought" represents the total claim of a given bank against all other members of the clearing house and nonmembers clearing through members. The completion of clearings involves (1) the physical exchange of checks between the various institutions and (2) the settlement of balances.[1] The total amount of checks brought by the participating banks is obviously identical with the total amount paid for; it is this amount that is reported as the daily "clearings" of a given center. Balances are settled not by individual pairs of banks, but between each bank and the manager of the clearing house, who represents all the other banks. Thus one single payment (originally in cash, later frequently in clearing house loan certificates, and now in most cases through entries on the books of the respective Federal Reserve Banks, or in smaller centers, by drafts on correspondent banks), which usually amounts to a small fraction of amounts exchanged, settles the total amount of exchange transactions of each bank with all other participating institutions.

In general, any payment made by drawing against a checking account or an interbank account may enter into the clearings figures if the drawee bank is a member of a local clearing house (in some cities clearing house banks act as agents in clearing items of one or several smaller commercial banks or of savings institutions) and if the check is not deposited with the drawee bank itself. In most cities clearing house associations exchange also some or all of the following items: drafts on railroads and large local business firms, State and county warrants, noncash collection items (such as coupons), and express money orders. Comparability between debits and clearings is normally not impaired by the clearing of items other than checks since remittances for these miscellaneous items are ultimately debited to deposit accounts at the various clearing house banks.

Clearings also include a considerable volume of drafts originating in interbank transactions and in portfolio adjustments of commercial banks. The interbank items include bank drafts against accounts with correspondent banks (including checks drawn in settlement of clearing house balances), drafts of member banks (and

---

[1] For details of the clearing procedure, see Walter E. Spahr, *The Clearing and Collection of Checks*, Chap. X.

of banks maintaining clearing accounts) against their balances at the Federal Reserve Banks, and checks issued by banks against themselves (certified and officers' checks, including salary, general expense, and dividend checks).

Local clearing house associations, which are the primary source of clearings statistics, vary greatly in the scope of their operations and in procedures used to settle balances.[2] In New York City and in some other large financial centers, clearing house associations have independent quarters and permanent salaried managers; they publish annual reports and maintain detailed historical records.[3] In other centers, where the functions of the clearing house manager are usually exercised in rotation by officials of the participating banks, frequent changes in management make investigation of unusual changes in clearings an arduous or even impossible undertaking. Even when historical records have been preserved, they are difficult to interpret without help from those who have had intimate contact with the underlying operations.

A comprehensive tabulation of clearings throughout the country is not available for years prior to 1884, although clearing house associations were established in several leading financial centers within a few years of the formation of the New York institution in 1853.[4] For this early period it has not even been possible to establish a reliable list of clearing houses operating in each individual year.

Prior to 1884-85, bank clearings were published by the leading trade and financial magazines such as *The Public* ("a weekly journal of finance, commercial interests, and political science"), *The Merchants Magazine*, and *The Bankers' Magazine* (which also published annually a review article on clearing houses). Since every magazine had to obtain statistical data directly from individual clearing houses, however, it is not surprising that the number of clearing houses for

---

[2] For historical material on the various activities of a local clearing house, see Jerome Thralls, *The Clearing House;* Spahr, *The Clearing and Collection of Checks,* particularly Chap. X. See also Dudley P. Bailey, "The Clearing House System," *The Bankers' Magazine,* February-June 1890, pp. 606-11, 660-69, 751-63, 845-52, and 917-18 for the early history of clearing house associations of the principal cities. These articles give a rather detailed description of the organization and procedures of all clearing houses established prior to 1889, and include annual statistics—for as many back years as available—on number of participating banks, volume of clearings and balances settled, and ratios of balances to clearings.

[3] Since the inauguration of the Federal Reserve System, some of the Federal Reserve Banks or their branches have provided office space and clerical help for conducting local check exchanges. Items presented by the Reserve Banks have come to represent a very large share of total exchanges in most cities in which Federal Reserve offices are located.

[4] The Boston Clearing House, which began to operate in 1855, was the first to be formed outside New York.

which the individual magazines carried data varied. *The Bankers' Magazine*, for example, gave 1875 data for only 10 clearing houses while *The Public* listed 16. Two years later *The Bankers' Magazine* listed 20 clearing houses while *The Public* included only 17. Comparison of the number of cities included in national totals for individual years with the list of centers in which clearing houses are known to have been in operation (see Table 1) suggests that the available tabulations did not include all active clearing house centers.[5]

TABLE 1

CLEARING HOUSES OUTSIDE NEW YORK CITY, SELECTED YEARS

Year	Number in operation	Number for which *annual* clearings are available[1]	Number included in Macaulay's *monthly* series[2]
1860	4	2	—
1865	7	4	—
1870	13	8	—
1875	22	14	9
1880	28	25	20
1885	34	34	27

[1] From a table in Dudley P. Bailey's "The Clearing House System," *The Bankers' Magazine*, June 1890, p. 917.

[2] For discussion of Macaulay's series, see below, pp. 15-16.

In 1884 the *Commercial and Financial Chronicle* (which had absorbed *The Public*) began to publish weekly and monthly tabulations for all clearing houses in operation.[6] The list of reporting centers increased continually from the original 26 included in the 1884 tabulations. Kansas City and San Francisco were the only two cities west of the Mississippi included in 1884, and in subsequent years the coverage of the rapidly growing western and southwestern areas of the country was improved.[7]

---

[5] The most convenient source for annual clearings for the years 1853 through 1877 is *The Bankers' Magazine*, 1890-91, p. 686; for the years 1878 through 1885, the *Financial Review*, 1886, p. 6.

[6] Summary tables of weekly data were started in the Oct. 4, 1884 issue and of monthly data in the Mar. 7, 1885 issue. Between 1891 and 1931 the *Annual Report of the Comptroller of the Currency* published in tabular form clearings for fiscal years ending September 30 of all centers reporting to the New York Clearing House Association.

[7] Edwin Frickey found that between 1875 and 1902 there were nine cases in which the clearings for individual cities added during a given year increased outside clearings for that year by one per cent or more. "Bank Clearings Outside New York City, 1875-1914," *Review of Economic Statistics*, October 1925, p. 252.

By the end of the century the number of reporting centers had increased to 87 and it reached its peak of 198 in 1920. The number of clearing houses operating throughout the country remained close to this maximum during the twenties, but declined from 191 to 172 between 1930 and 1932. As of April 1958, clearings for 179 individual cities were tabulated by the *Chronicle*.

It has sometimes been claimed that clearings figures are unreliable because of duplications resulting from the passage of checks through more than one clearing house.[8] Actually, this can happen only if a city clearing house operates a subsidiary organization usually called a "country clearing house" for the collection of items drawn on banks in the surrounding territory.[9] Double counting then results because the country checks collected are included in clearings on one day and the remittances received for them on the following day. The only other normal source of duplication arises from cashiers' checks issued for items that have been dishonored or returned for some other reason; the amounts involved, however, are relatively small.[10]

Instances have been cited of the padding of clearing house statistics in order to create the impression of growing activity or to make a more favorable comparison with totals for a rival city. The *Chronicle*, in the course of its long preoccupation with clearings statistics, found that such padding had taken place mainly in the smaller centers. The most common technique was to report both sides of the clearing sheet, thus doubling the totals.[11] Normally only a few weeks or months would pass before such a deception was discovered. More subtle padding—such as an artificial increase in check circulation with the cooperation of large depositors—was more

---

[8] For instance, Ray B. Westerfield, *Money, Credit and Banking*, p. 269; W. Randolph Burgess, "Velocity of Bank Deposits," *Journal of the American Statistical Association*, June 1923, p. 728; and Spahr, *The Clearing and Collection of Checks*, pp. 483-84.

[9] The first such country clearing house was organized in Boston in 1899, and in the following years similar collection arrangements were made in about a dozen additional cities. Their number and importance declined with the creation of the Federal Reserve clearing system. For details, see Spahr, *The Clearing and Collection of Checks*, pp. 126-28.

[10] Before facilities for rapid transfer of funds became available through the organization of the Federal Reserve System, some smaller clearing houses did not require that daily balances be settled in cash; instead, managers issued drafts against members with passive balances. These drafts were recleared the following day. Thus, each day's clearings included balances resulting from the previous day's check exchanges. In clearing houses with a small number of participating banks, debit balances may have been relatively large in relation to the amounts of checks exchanged.

[11] See, for instance, the *Journal of the American Bankers Association*, February 1913, p. 504. As indicated by the November 1913 issue of this *Journal*, p. 341, the Clearing House Section of the American Bankers Association fought vigorously against such misrepresentations.

difficult to detect. The *Chronicle* concluded that "this spirit of provincialism exists only at minor and unimportant places, and finds no tolerance in larger communities . . . of real consequence."[12]

In some cases, however, local clearing practices have the effect of raising the amount of clearings reported. Thus, in a leading center in the East clearing banks estimate the approximate amount of their adverse balances and send through the clearing house drafts on their reserve accounts in order to come out about even when balances are struck at the clearing house. As a consequence, clearings are immediately increased by the amount of the estimated adverse balances.

While it is probably true that willful distortion of clearings has occurred only temporarily and in small localities—it is claimed that this happened particularly in the West—published aggregates for the country as a whole have from time to time been affected by suspension of publication of figures by clearing houses, mainly in centers that have experienced a decline in their exchanges.[13]

Creation of the Federal Reserve System has on balance increased the volume of commercial checks exchanged in Federal Reserve and branch cities, although it also has caused a relative decrease in the circulation of bank drafts for the purpose of adjusting reserves and interbank balances.

Operations of the Federal Reserve System began to be reflected in the volume of clearings even before the nationwide Federal Reserve clearing and collection system began to operate. The New York Federal Reserve Bank became a member of the clearing house in November 1914 soon after being chartered, and the volume of the Bank's exchanges became considerable after it began to collect country items throughout the Second Federal Reserve District. The Boston Reserve Bank became a member of the local clearing house in the same month.

With the establishment of the Gold Settlement Fund for clearing payments between the Federal Reserve Banks in May 1915, the way was opened for an interdistrict as well as an intradistrict clearing system. After a not too successful experimentation with a voluntary

---

[12] Mar. 11, 1922, p. 989.

[13] The most important city that has not been included in the *Chronicle* tabulations since 1932 is Los Angeles, which in 1957 was the fourth largest clearing center in the country.

clearing system within the individual Federal Reserve districts, and with a modified "compulsory" plan, the Federal Reserve collection and clearing system became fully effective only after the concentration of reserves in the Reserve Banks was completed by July 1917. An attempt was made at the same time to increase the scope of the Federal Reserve clearing system by making system facilities available to nonmember banks remitting at par, but the number of banks availing themselves of this opportunity never became large.[14]

The Federal Reserve collection and clearing system was gradually integrated with the older system of local and country clearing houses. The Reserve Banks and their branches gradually became regular or special (limited) members (depending on local conditions and requirements of clearing house memberships) of the local clearing houses. Some of the Reserve Banks (Minneapolis, Dallas) and branches (Buffalo, Birmingham, Jacksonville, Nashville, Little Rock, Louisville, Memphis, Oklahoma City, El Paso, and Houston) joined local clearing houses as late as 1919 or 1920. The *Financial Review* estimated that Reserve Banks and their branches that had become members of local clearing houses in 1920 alone had increased the volume of reported exchanges for that year by $3.5 billion or almost 2 per cent of total outside clearings (while changes in methods of compiling at a few smaller clearing houses added another $500 million).[15] In some cases, the participation of Federal Reserve offices raised local clearings immediately to a multiple of their previous level.

Participation of the Reserve Banks and their branches in local clearings has resulted in the clearing of a larger proportion of items drawn on local banks and deposited out of town, since all such checks collected through the Reserve Banks are cleared.[16] Some checks collected through city correspondents, on the other hand, are drawn on them and need not be presented through the clearing

---

[14] For a more detailed discussion of the organization and expansion of the Federal Reserve clearing and collection system, see Spahr, *The Clearing and Collection of Checks*, pp. 164-231 and 528-81.

[15] The *Financial Review* (annual supplement to the *Commercial and Financial Chronicle*), 1921, p. 122.

[16] The Federal Reserve Bank of Chicago presents checks on clearing house banks directly; it clears only checks on 12 banks affiliated with the clearing house (six of which are located outside the City of Chicago proper) and on 56 other banks in outlying sections that participate in clearings by receiving checks from the clearing house banks but do not present checks for clearing. Furthermore, the Federal Reserve Bank of Chicago receives through the clearing house only return items and daily settlement drafts drawn upon it by from 35 to 40 of the non-affiliated members which it sponsors; banks present Treasury checks and Federal Reserve drafts to the Reserve Bank over the counter. The limited use made of the local clearing house by the Federal Reserve Bank of Chicago goes a long way toward explaining why Chicago clearings are small relative to the size and commercial and financial importance of the city.

house. Nevertheless, the very sharp increases which occurred in many centers after the Reserve Banks (or their branches) began to participate in local exchanges exaggerated the importance of the change. After the Federal Reserve collection system began to operate, the volume of local exchanges declined because correspondent banks lost some of their collection business while Federal Reserve Banks and branches collected on local banks by direct presentation. Consequently, percentage increases in clearings following the inclusion of the Federal Reserve exchanges were measured from temporarily reduced levels.

While the percentage of *checks* deposited out of town that pass through local clearings has increased considerably since the inauguration of the Federal Reserve clearing system, the circulation and clearing of *bank drafts* has declined. The Federal Reserve System has gradually expanded its facilities for the wire transfer of funds for member banks and their customers and for the adjustment on the books of the Federal Reserve Banks of balances of out-of-town clearing houses (which otherwise would have been adjusted by drafts against balances with correspondent banks, usually in New York).[17] The subsequent development of private wire systems by several leading banks culminating in 1950 in the inauguration of the nationwide Bank Wire System had a similar effect. All these facilities have considerably reduced the need for transferring bank funds by draft. In a general way, the centralization of reserves in the Federal Reserve Banks has had the effect of reducing the circulation (and clearing) of drafts for the purpose of adjusting reserve positions; reserves can be shifted among member banks by simple book entries on the books of the respective Federal Reserve Banks. As a result of all these developments, the ratio of clearings to debits has declined, although irregularly, ever since 1919, as discussed more fully in Chapter IV.

In current monetary and business analysis, clearings have been almost completely superseded by debits. Since revision of the debits data in 1953 (see pages 32-33), however, clearings remain the only *weekly* data on the flow of payments. Since 1947, Dun and Brad-

---

[17] In the middle of 1953, balances of 13 city clearing houses in the New York District, 20 in the Philadelphia District, and smaller numbers in several other districts were adjusted on the books of the Reserve Banks. Corresponding arrangements for a total of 47 county clearing plans (check exchanges among banks in a given county) existed in the New York and Philadelphia Districts, while several other Reserve Banks or branches made book transfers of credits for clearings in distant cities, but on a much smaller scale.

street has been publishing every Thursday weekly clearings for leading centers outside New York City (24 beginning in 1947 and 25 since May 1954), as well as figures for New York City. An examination of monthly totals derived from these data shows a close correlation with monthly debits to demand deposit accounts for the outside centers. Because of this correlation, some use is being made of weekly clearings, with proper adjustment for holidays and split weeks at month-end, for projecting debits for the current month before the official totals are released.

OUTSIDE CLEARINGS SERIES

In order to obtain a comprehensive long-run series of clearings, one might proceed in any one of three ways: (1) use a constant sample of cities, (2) use the aggregate clearings of all reporting centers and adjust for the bias resulting from increasing numbers of reporting clearing centers, or (3) use the aggregate clearings of all centers for which data are available. The first course was followed by Edwin Frickey of Harvard University, the second by Frederick R. Macaulay of the National Bureau of Economic Research, and the third by Carl Snyder of the Federal Reserve Bank of New York. In all three cases, a national series excluding New York clearings (which, because of their sensitivity to financial transactions, are usually analyzed separately) was computed.

Frickey started out by studying the monthly clearings for the period 1903-13 of 17 selected large cities outside New York City whose bank clearings for the year 1910 constituted as much as one per cent of total "outside" clearings, as compiled by the *Chronicle*.[18] After eliminating data for four cities because they showed either no appreciable cyclical fluctuations, large and irregular fluctuations, or sudden shifts in level, and another six cities because "their cyclical fluctuations were either quite unlike those for total outside clearings or not sufficiently similar to justify inclusion in the index," Frickey retained seven cities—Baltimore, Chicago, Cincinnati, Cleveland,

---

[18] Frickey, *Review of Economic Statistics*, October 1925, pp. 252-62. See also the May 1930 issue of the *Review*, pp. 90-99, for Frickey's "A Statistical Study of Bank Clearings, 1875-1914." Monthly series for each of the seven cities are given in William L. Crum and Alson C. Patton, *An Introduction to Methods of Economic Statistics*, pp. 447-57.

Frickey later extended this series back to 1866, but on a quarterly basis only, using annual data for six cities, four of which are included in the series which begins in 1875. Clearings for Philadelphia alone were used as an interpolater in order to obtain quarterly data. See Frickey, *Economic Fluctuations in the United States*, pp. 360-61. Actual data for 1866-74, however, are not tabulated in this source.

TABLE 2

MONTHLY OUTSIDE CLEARINGS SERIES

Compiler	Coverage	Period	Remarks
Commercial and Financial Chronicle[1]	All reporting centers	1884 to date	Monthly totals
Frickey[2]	Seven cities	1875-1914	Monthly totals
Macaulay[3]	All reporting centers, raised to 1919 level	1875-1918	Daily averages of monthly figures

[1] 1885 and subsequent years. Current and year-ago data published regularly. Extended back to 1875 by Snyder but not published.
[2] "Bank Clearings Outside New York City, 1875-1914," *Review of Economic Statistics*, October 1925, pp. 252-62. See also text footnote 18 on the preceding page.
[3] *Some Theoretical Problems Suggested by the Movements of Interest Rates, Bond Yields, and Stock Prices in the United States since 1856*, pp. A255-65.

Philadelphia, Pittsburgh, and San Francisco. Aggregate clearings for these seven cities paralleled total outside clearings very closely during the period studied by Frickey. Actually, clearings for two financial centers dominate this series, accounting for about two-thirds of the aggregate. Thus in 1877 clearings for Philadelphia constituted 40 per cent and those for Chicago 23 per cent of the seven-city aggregate; in 1902, Philadelphia's share had dropped to 28 per cent, but that of Chicago had increased to 40 per cent.

The alternative series compiled by Macaulay is based on all clearings data available for each year.[19] Working backward from clearings reported at the end of 1918, Macaulay raised progressively the level of clearings reported for earlier years by chaining totals for all clearing houses operating outside New York in a given year. Macaulay's adjustments involved making the percentage movement of the raised series from each December to the immediately succeeding January the same as the percentage movement of the totals of the largest number of cities whose clearings were available for both December and the following January. By this procedure the level of the adjusted series was raised progressively for the early years above the totals actually reported. For 1875, when Macaulay's series starts, the level of the blown-up series is 41 per cent higher than reported clearings for that year. Macaulay's estimates of monthly or annual totals have never been published, but daily averages of monthly clearings outside New York City (as well as a corresponding

[19] Frederick R. Macaulay, *Some Theoretical Problems Suggested by the Movements of Interest Rates, Bond Yields, and Stock Prices in the United States since 1856*.

15

series for New York City beginning in October 1853) are available in the volume cited in footnote 19.

A third alternative is the series of aggregate outside clearings exactly as published in the *Commercial and Financial Chronicle* and, prior to 1884, in various financial publications. Such a series was used by Snyder, who held that the gradual addition of data for new clearing houses to United States totals reflected primarily the economic growth of the country.[20] Among the centers that have been added since 1875, when his compilation begins, the rapidly growing commercial and financial centers of the Middle West, Southwest, and Pacific Coast far outweighed the relatively minor clearing centers in long-settled areas of the East. Since Snyder was interested in the underlying long-run forces of economic growth no less than in the cyclical fluctuations of economic activity, he preferred the unadjusted series whose long-run trend reflected the gradual expansion of the active economic area of the country.

For a study of cyclical fluctuations, Macaulay's series is clearly preferable since it eliminates random upward shifts in the level of the series such as might have resulted from time to time from the addition of one or several new clearing houses. If, however, the long-run rate of growth (or comparison of the volume of New York with that of outside clearings) rather than the cyclical pattern is to be investigated, Macaulay's series has serious limitations. His data for 1875, for instance, are no more than an estimate of the amount of checks that would have been exchanged in that year if all the centers which initiated clearing arrangements during 1876-1918 had initiated them before 1875. Some of the centers thus allowed for were rather small communities in 1875, but they were given an importance in that year commensurate with the relative significance of their clearings in December of the first year in which they became available.

Frickey's series reflects the composite secular growth of seven cities (two of which account for about two-thirds of the total), not that of the country as a whole. Furthermore, it is heavily weighted by the old industrial centers of the East and Middle West. San

---

[20] Carl Snyder, "A New Clearings Index of Business for Fifty Years," *Journal of the American Statistical Association*, September 1924, pp. 329-35. See also his *Business Cycles and Business Measurements*, Chap. VI.

Francisco is the only city included that is located west of Chicago or south of Cincinnati. Snyder's series based on all reporting centers is clearly to be preferred for studies of trends in the volume of clearings, even though its rate of growth is somewhat exaggerated by the lack of back data for some centers added after 1875.

NEW YORK CLEARINGS

Prior to World War II, New York clearings alone exceeded those of all other reporting centers combined.[21] But the justification for the separate treatment of New York clearings lies not so much in their absolute size as in the degree to which they reflect financial transactions. In the remainder of the country, clearings represent essentially business and personal transactions. The New York series has been used widely to represent "speculation" rather than "business."[22] Although financial transactions also enter into the clearings of other centers, the preponderant position of the New York Stock Exchange and the concentration of other financial institutions in New York explain the large contribution of financial clearings to the totals for that city. They also explain some of the divergencies between the cyclical movements of the series for New York and the series for the rest of the country.

The impact of transactions at the New York Stock Exchange—the largest organized security market in the country—on the volume of New York clearings has been conspicuous. When starting the regular publication of clearings statistics in 1884, the *Chronicle* pointed out that clearings in general are "but an imperfect indication of the activity of legitimate business, especially in New York and some of the western cities. This is chiefly due to speculative operations, which at the Stock Exchange and in leading centers so decidedly outnumber actual transactions, and which may be as large or larger in the midst of general depression and on a declining market as in good times and a rising market."[23] In discussing fluctuations in clearings, the *Chronicle* frequently compared outside

---

[1] For convenient monthly tabulations of New York clearings for 1866-1914, see *Review of Economic Statistics*, October 1926, p. 188, and January 1919, p. 64; for 1866 to 1883 the monthly totals were computed from weekly data. For October 1854 through January 1919, a monthly series of daily averages of New York clearings is available in Macaulay's *Interest Rates, Bond Yields, and Stock Prices*, pp. A253-66.

[22] A rather detailed description of changes in the membership and procedures of the New York Clearing House is given in Appendix I of the first edition of this publication.

[23] Issue of Oct. 4, 1884, p. 359.

17

clearings with New York clearings reduced by double the amount of the value of stock sales.[24] These sales, as well as the volume of trading in grains, cotton, and petroleum at the various New York commodity exchanges, were published by the *Chronicle* for a number of years along with its figures on New York clearings.[25]

The important contribution of stock exchange transactions to New York clearings was clearly demonstrated at the outbreak of World War I when the New York Stock Exchange was closed temporarily. While outside clearings had been only about half the amount of New York clearings prior to the closing, they exceeded the latter by a substantial margin for several weeks after the closing. With the resumption of Stock Exchange trading the old proportion was immediately restored.

All attempts to ascertain precisely the share of speculative transactions in New York clearings met with the insurmountable difficulty of inadequate statistics. Economists who approached the subject could do little more than take notice of the importance of speculative transactions in the total volume of check payments in New York City and illustrate their point by showing the inter-relationship between the amount of shares sold on the New York Stock Exchange and New York clearings.[26]

The contribution to clearings of payments arising from securities trading at the New York Stock Exchange and at various other local security exchanges depended not only on the activity of these markets, but also on the institutional arrangements made from time to time to reduce the volume of payments arising from securities trading. The techniques of delivering securities, making payments for securities purchased, offsetting various types of intermediate transactions, and making "street loans" and other money transactions incident to trading in securities have been subject to numerous changes.[27] While

---

[24] In its annual reviews of "clearings and speculation" it carried during the nineties a table on New York clearings less 2½ times stock sales at the New York Stock Exchange. See, for instance, the issue for Jan. 9, 1892, p. 51.

[25] During the last quarter of the nineteenth century, New York was a large market for crude petroleum; the first pipeline reached the Atlantic Coast at Bayonne, N. J. in 1879, and an active speculation in pipeline certificates developed at several New York stock exchanges.

[26] See, for instance, Wesley C. Mitchell, *Business Cycles*, chart on p. 249. For an early attempt to investigate statistically the degree to which stock exchange trading and other forms of speculation affect the volume of New York clearings and their fluctuations, see Norman J. Silberling, "The Mystery of Clearings," *The Annalist*, Aug. 14, 1916. This article was apparently written under Professor B. M. Anderson's guidance while the author was a student at Harvard.

[27] While the Big Board has always dominated securities trading in New York City, several rival organizations have existed at different times, in particular during the second half of the nineteenth century. Of

the influence of the numerous changes in customs and rules which have regulated stock trading at the New York Stock Exchange (and its various rivals) cannot be traced in detail, one institutional change —the establishment of the Clearing House of the New York Stock Exchange (later known as the Stock Clearing Corporation)—had a considerable and lasting effect on the volume of check clearings which will be discussed briefly.

As early as 1880, and probably even earlier, some minor economies in the use of checks in securities trading resulted from the direct offsetting of certain transactions by members of the Exchange who undertook, for a fee, to clear stock for other members. In May 1892, after earlier plans had failed, a stock clearing house was established by the New York Stock Exchange for the purpose of clearing purchases and sales in a limited number of particularly active securities. Gradual elimination of delivery of an increasingly large number of securities, which was achieved by offsetting transactions among the members of the Stock Exchange Clearing House (which counted among its members all important Stock Exchange firms), reduced the circulation of checks and therefore the amount of check exchanges at the New York Clearing House.[28]

The amount of check payments obviated by the operations of the Stock Clearing House, renamed the Stock Clearing Corporation in 1920, has increased gradually as the list of securities cleared has been lengthened and, after 1920, as new types of transactions have been added. The greatest reduction in check payments (and consequently clearings) thus achieved was in 1920, when the clearing of money payments by the "day branch" was inaugurated. Since 1921 the operation of the Stock Clearing Corporation has replaced payment by check in amounts ranging from less than $10 billion to more than $100 billion a year. If checks for such amounts had been cleared—which would have been likely in the absence of the Stock Clearing Corporation—New York clearings for 1921 to 1946 would have been increased on the average by about 12 per cent.

---

these, only the Curb Exchange survives. The modes of operation of the various competing exchanges and of the informal open-air stock market out of which the Curb Exchange finally emerged differed in many respects from that of the Big Board. The combined volume of business of all the minor exchanges has probably never exceeded that of the New York Stock Exchange, but at times it was far from negligible. See George Garvy, "Rivals and Interlopers in the History of the New York Security Market," *Journal of Political Economy*, June 1944, pp. 128-43.

[28] Mitchell suggested this as early as 1913 in his *Business Cycles*, p. 247.

Another element in the reduction of check clearings is the fact that checks in payment of stock clearing balances are drawn against a small number of downtown banks. Consequently, some of these remittances do not reach the New York Clearing House but give rise to book entries only.

While it is not possible to determine precisely how much check payments (and clearings) originating in financial transactions have been reduced by the operation of the Stock Clearing Corporation and by similar arrangements at other local stock exchanges, it is certain that clearings arising from a given volume of security transactions were gradually reduced after 1892 and even more so after 1920. Most of these economies in check circulation, however, were achieved in transactions among brokers. Payments between principals and brokers, which because of margin trading and for other reasons account for the smaller part of all payments arising from stock trading, were hardly reduced at all. Also, the *proportion* of checks exchanged that originated in financial transactions need not have been reduced in relation to total New York clearings—particularly between 1892 and 1929—since the amount of securities transactions is likely to have increased more than transactions arising from the production and distribution of goods and services.

Similar arrangements for reducing the circulation of checks by offsetting money payments were also developed by several New York commodity exchanges before the turn of the century.[29] The amounts involved, however, were considerably smaller than at the Stock Exchange. Also, before such arrangements were formalized by the formation of clearing associations, the amounts of money payments were considerably reduced by "ringing out" sales (netting out offsetting transactions). It is therefore not possible to estimate with any degree of reliability at what precise time and to what extent the volume of check payments was reduced by any of the several money-clearing arrangements in existence at several New York commodity exchanges, but it is unlikely that the amounts involved were ever comparable in volume to the reductions made by the New York Stock Clearing Corporation.[30]

---

[29] See p. 66, footnote 2.

[30] Just before the establishment of the Stock Clearing House the *Commercial and Financial Chronicle* (Jan. 9, 1892) commented, after pointing to the effect of increased stock exchange activity on New York

While it is not possible to estimate with any degree of reliability the share of total payments arising from stock exchange and related trading, it can be shown indirectly that the contribution of such check payments to New York clearings was considerable. In the chart on page 22, New York clearings for 1875-1919 are expressed as a ratio of (1) clearings outside New York City adjusted for upward drift (Macaulay's series) and (2) clearings in seven leading cities outside New York (Frickey's series). The estimated dollar value of stocks sold on the New York Stock Exchange is shown in the lower part of the chart.[31] The movement of the ratio of New York to outside clearings supports strongly the generally accepted view that the New York series has been considerably affected by the value of stock exchange transactions.

Between 1878 and 1881 the estimated dollar value of stock sales nearly quadrupled while the ratio of New York to outside clearings increased from 2.1 to 3.0. In subsequent years, as the estimated value of stock sales at the New York Stock Exchange declined, this ratio declined to a low point of 1.1 (in 1894). In the period between 1894 and 1901 there was a very rapid expansion of stock trading, accompanied by increased activity in other types of financial transactions related to the rapid growth of corporate enterprise and numerous business reorganizations and mergers.[32] The dollar volume of stock sales is estimated to have increased fivefold in this seven-year period and the ratio of New York to outside clearings nearly doubled (increasing from 1.1 to 2.0). Thus the ratio increased in about the same proportion to the increase in the volume of stock sales as during the previous period of rapid increase in stock trading, 1878-81. From 1906 to 1914 both the volume of stock sales on the Stock Exchange and the ratio of New York to outside clearings declined irregularly. During the entire period 1875-1919 most of the marked reversals in the movement of the estimated dollar volume of New York stock

clearings: "On the Produce Exchange the year was one of very heavy business, but the effect in that case on clearings is comparatively unimportant, since the Produce Exchange clears its own transactions."

[31] For the period prior to World War I, the most useful continuous data related to the activity in New York financial markets are the series on the total value of stock sales at the New York Stock Exchange estimated by the *Chronicle* by multiplying the number of shares sold by their average price. This series is probably on the whole representative of the direction and amplitude of cyclical fluctuations in the dollar volume of stock trading, but not of the total amount of payments arising from financial transactions. It does not cover sales at other stock exchanges that have been active in the city at various times, over-the-counter trading, etc.

[32] Withdrawal of New York trust companies from clearings after 1903 did not seem to have any marked effect on the ratio, nor did their return in 1911 interrupt the gradual decline in clearings which occurred between 1909 and 1914.

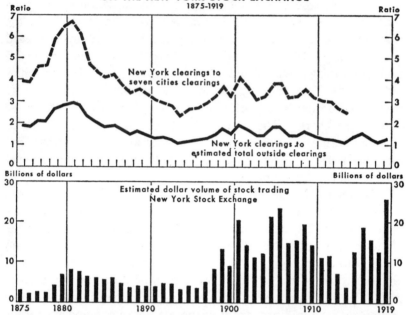

Chart I

**RATIO OF NEW YORK CITY CLEARINGS TO OUTSIDE CLEARINGS
AND THE ESTIMATED DOLLAR VOLUME OF STOCK TRADING
ON THE NEW YORK STOCK EXCHANGE**

1875-1919

Sources.—New York clearings: 1875-79—*The Public*; 1880-1919—*Commercial and Financial Chronicle.*
Outside clearings: F. R. Macaulay's unpublished estimates. Seven cities' clearings: E. Frickey, *Review of Economic Statistics*, October 1925, p. 260. Value of shares sold on the New York Stock Exchange: *Commercial and Financial Chronicle.*

sales (1886, 1900, 1904-06, 1908-09, and 1914-16) were reflected in a corresponding reversal in the ratio between the two clearings series.[33]

The ratios between New York clearings and the Frickey series for seven leading cities exhibit almost the same fluctuations as the first set of ratios. Since the seven-cities series covers only about half of the amount of clearings represented by the Macaulay series, these ratios are about twice as large. The close correspondence in fluctuations of the two series of ratios indicates that—compared with New York—the share of financial transactions in total clearings of the seven large cities has been relatively small. Otherwise, a simultaneous increase in financial clearings in these cities and in New York would

---

[33] From 1923 to 1929 the increase of the ratio (from 1.1 to 1.9) was similar to increases observed during the spurts in stock exchange activity in 1878-81 and 1894-1901, although the increase in the volume of stock sales was much sharper than in the earlier periods.

tend to wipe out the peaks in the ratio shown by the more inclusive series in periods of increased stock exchange activity in New York.

As will be shown in the following chapter, financial transactions continued after World War I to contribute heavily to aggregate check payments, but their exact share in New York debits is as difficult to estimate as their share in New York clearings prior to 1918.

On the other hand, changes in the national collection system and in the scope of operations of the New York Clearing House have affected New York clearings relatively little during the period of nearly 100 years for which they are available.

Clearing of checks and drafts on New York banks is to a large extent the final step in the nationwide collection process built up on a web of correspondent relationships upon which the Federal Reserve System has been superimposed. Changes in correspondent relationships, in collection channels and techniques, and in bank accounting procedures have been taking place continuously.[34] In general the net result has been a reduction of the amount of interbank payments involved. The fluidity of all collection and clearing arrangements and the continued search for simpler and more expedient procedures have made for gradual rather than sudden change.

Changes in the rules and regulations of the New York Clearing House had by themselves relatively little effect on the volume of checks cleared. The provision limiting membership of the Clearing House to institutions with a certain minimum capitalization did not materially restrict the volume of New York clearings. It simply vested the management of the Clearing House in the hands of the stronger banks without excluding other institutions from the benefits of participation in check exchanges. At all times, the larger downtown banks accounted for the bulk of the volume of checks exchanged.

The development of new collection mechanisms, such as the country and city collection departments of the Clearing House Association and the Federal Reserve collection system, brought a certain amount of additional items through the clearing house. To a certain extent these new collection arrangements involved only a

---

[34] Thus the agreement entered into by the New York banks in 1899 to charge for collection of out-of-town checks channeled a larger part of country checks to other eastern centers and reduced the volume of remittance drafts cleared in New York. See Spahr, *The Clearing and Collection of Checks*, p. 126.

change in the channels through which checks reached the clearing house, so that the total dollar volume of clearings was neither reduced nor increased. As these changes in city and country collection arrangements coincided with World War I, it is practically impossible to ascertain their impact statistically. Changes in collection, transit, and money transfer methods following the inauguration of the Federal Reserve System were of considerable importance but they gained momentum only after the end of World War I when the debits series became available and the clearings series lost much of its usefulness. The use of the facilities of the Federal Reserve System by its members—and the efficiency with which the facilities were operated—developed slowly and so all changes worked out gradually.

In the long run and cyclically, the fluctuating share of clearings arising from stock market activities has influenced New York clearings to a much larger extent than have any changes in the structure and membership of the organization itself. While changes in membership and procedure (notably after the turn of the century) have caused the volume of clearings to increase or to decrease, on the whole the resulting changes in the level of clearings or in their rate of increase must have been relatively small, in many cases negligible.

For the 40-year period from 1853 to about 1892 (covered by relatively few economic time series) New York clearings, although particularly heavily weighted by financial transactions, included consistently all drafts and checks exchanged by practically all banks operating in the greater New York area. In subsequent years, the volume of clearings arising from Stock Exchange trading was reduced through the gradual extension of stock clearing. As has been indicated above, however, it is questionable whether on balance the impact of financial transactions on New York clearings has diminished.

III. Debits Statistics

For many years, debits have been used in preference to clearings in current business and monetary analysis. Since the Federal Reserve began collection of debits statistics, several major changes have been made in the scope, coverage, and frequency of the published series. In this chapter the development of the several debits series no longer published is reviewed; then, the debits series currently published as a result of the consolidation of the monthly and weekly series in 1953 is discussed. Finally, the special factors affecting New York debits are discussed.

The first attempt to collect debits data goes back to 1908 when the Clearing House Section of the American Bankers Association (ABA), at its annual meeting, adopted a resolution to "recommend that each bank report weekly to the manager of the clearing house in its own city the total of all checks on itself charged on its books, except cashiers' checks given in payment of clearing house balances." Several years passed before an appreciable number of clearing houses started collecting and reporting debits statistics. These reports were collected largely through the effort of O. Howard Wolfe, then Secretary of the Clearing House Section of the American Bankers Association.[1]

Prior to 1916 the number of clearing houses that collected debits was so small and the reports so irregular that the data were not made public by the ABA. About 100 clearing houses at different times attempted the compilation of weekly debits figures, but only 29 reported usable figures regularly enough to permit compilation and release of quarterly totals by 1916. These data included debits to interbank accounts as well as debits to individual accounts. In July

---

[1] A comparison of "total bank transactions" (as bank debits were originally called) with clearings showed that in the 22 centers outside New York which reported from June 1913 to November 1914 clearings averaged only about 40 per cent of all debits against deposit liabilities (including bank balances). See *The Annalist*, Dec. 7, 1914, for a list of these centers and a weekly chart of these aggregate debits and clearings. *The Annalist* commented: "When the fluctuations for a given city are taken separately, it is found that known events are not reflected to anything like the extent, or with the same accuracy in clearings, as in total transactions. At the time of the Cincinnati flood, for instance, clearings showed comparatively little change, while total transactions sharply reflected the fall in payroll money drawn from the banks and the general depression of business."

1918 the Clearing House Section of the ABA made a last effort to enlist the cooperation of the then existing 229 local clearing house associations. Inasmuch as only about a dozen additional centers agreed to report, the ABA decided to abandon its own collection of debits statistics and to cooperate in a project being started by the Federal Reserve Board.[2]

DEBITS TO TOTAL DEPOSIT ACCOUNTS

The Federal Reserve Board, which had been considering the matter for some time, began collecting debits for the week ended August 15, 1918.[3] Under the cooperative arrangements for the collection of debits which were originally made between the Federal Reserve Board and the Clearing House Section of the ABA, the compilation of totals for individual centers was left to the local clearing house managers, who then reported totals only to the respective Federal Reserve Banks which in their turn forwarded them to the Board. This automatic exclusion of banks that were not members (or at least clearing nonmembers) of the local clearing houses was subsequently formalized by specific instructions of the Federal Reserve Board.

Unlike data previously collected by the ABA, the initial Federal Reserve tabulations carried separate data for debits (1) to individual accounts and (2) to banks and bankers' accounts.[4] By the end of

---

[2] For a comprehensive account of the efforts of the Clearing House Section of the ABA in the form of a statement by Jerome Thralls, Secretary of that Section, see "Report of Total Bank Transactions," *Federal Reserve Bulletin*, September 1918, pp. 821-28. Half-year totals of debits ("total bank transactions," which include debits to interbank as well as debits to individual accounts) for 1917 and the first half of 1918 are also given for 29 individual centers, together with comparable clearings figures. Similar data for 27 of these cities for the first half of 1916 are available in Thralls, *The Clearing House*, pp. 56-57. Prior to 1918 the ABA data for three of these cities include also debits at Federal Reserve Banks.

[3] All the pertinent statements and letters by Federal Reserve authorities relative to the establishment of the new series, its purpose, coverage, and mode of compilation, are reproduced in full in the *Bulletin* article cited in the preceding footnote. See also Walter E. Spahr, *The Clearing and Collection of Checks*, pp. 487-89. A short description and history of the Board's series is given in *Banking and Monetary Statistics*, pp. 230-33.

[4] The original name of the series, "debits to individual accounts," apparently reflected the terminology used prior to 1935 in the call reports of the Comptroller of the Currency. From 1923 to 1935 the Federal Reserve Board also used the term "individual deposits" in its *Abstract of Condition of Member Banks* and in other reports. The name of the series was changed in 1940 to "debits to deposit accounts," and in 1942 to "debits to total deposit accounts except interbank accounts."

The collection of debits to interbank accounts was discontinued after the week ended Jan. 16, 1919. See *Federal Reserve Bulletin*, September 1919, p. 878.

Debits to interbank accounts were also collected from weekly reporting member banks for the period from the week ended Sept. 5, 1934 to the week ended Feb. 1, 1939, for use in the studies by the staff of the Board of Governors mentioned in Chap. VII, p. 99. Tabulations for New York and totals for all other weekly reporting banks are available in the files of the Board of Governors and were used in the preparation of the present study.

An analysis of these data for 1936 shows extremely large differences in the annual rates of turnover (ranging from 0.3 to 329.8 at individual banks), but it was felt that these variations reflected in part differences in remitting and accounting practices.

1918, reports were received from about 150 centers, or only about two-thirds of all clearing houses operating in the United States.[5] The number of reporting centers increased slowly to 167 at the end of 1921, more than three years after the inauguration of the new series. The Board subsequently announced that, beginning with the week ended February 1, 1922, it would publish debits to individual accounts for "all the centers of the United States where clearing house associations have been established, provided reports reach the Board in time for inclusion in its weekly statement."[6] The number of centers for which debits were released weekly was then increased to about 230. During the subsequent 14 years it grew gradually to 274 and remained practically unchanged from 1934 to May 1942.

The *Federal Reserve Bulletin* beginning with the September 1918 issue carried weekly data for all individual reporting centers, together with district and national totals.[7] Subsequently, after the inauguration of a special release, the amount of detail given in the *Bulletin* was gradually reduced and after April 1927 only monthly totals were published.

Since the number of cities for which current debits statistics were collected increased rapidly in the early twenties, a need was felt for a continuous series covering identical centers. The Federal Reserve Board consequently published in its *Annual Report* for 1921 a monthly series for 141 cities for which comparable data were available back to the beginning of 1919 and in 1923 began to publish this series currently in the *Federal Reserve Bulletin*. District totals as well as a breakdown of the national total between New York City and the other 140 cities were also given. Totals for weeks beginning in one month and ending in another were prorated on the basis of the number of business days falling in each month.[8] The problem of prorating split weeks raised numerous technical questions arising, among other things, from the incidence of holidays and from chang-

---

[5] The term "center" rather than "city" is used, as in some cases debits in adjacent communities are included. A few minor substitutions in the reporting centers included in the national series became necessary in the course of time. For details, see *Banking and Monetary Statistics*, p. 231. For additional historical and background information see *Federal Reserve Bulletin* for September 1918, pp. 821-28 and March 1919, p. 258; also Spahr, *The Clearing and Collection of Checks*, pp. 483-89, and sources cited therein.

[6] *Federal Reserve Bulletin*, March 1922, p. 358.

[7] The first report was for the week ended Aug. 15, 1918 and included a number of centers for which debits to interbank accounts were included with debits to individual accounts.

[8] See *Federal Reserve Bulletin*, July 1924, p. 555.

ing numbers of Sundays in a month. This monthly series was continued until the 1953 revision.[9]

Prior to the 1942 revisions, the weekly debits to total deposit accounts for an individual center (and consequently for the national totals) may have been subject to any or all of the following factors: (1) noncooperation of some clearing house banks, mostly during the earlier years; (2) reporting of incorrect totals by clearing house managers; and (3) changes in the banking structure. The influence of this third factor, of course, continued after the 1942 and 1953 revisions.

1. In several large centers, reporting for clearing house banks was not complete when the debits series was started. Some banks that were not members of the Federal Reserve System did not report until several years later. In some cases, belated cooperation subsequently increased the amounts reported by substantial amounts. Some of the most important instances of increased participation in reporting were mentioned in footnotes to tables published periodically in the *Federal Reserve Bulletin* and in other Federal Reserve publications.[10] It is not certain, however, that all increases in the coverage of the data for individual cities were so indicated. The largest single change that could be traced as a result of the more complete reporting of banks within the city of Boston lifted the national series for 140 centers (excluding New York City) by no more than 2 per cent. The aggregate effect of under-reporting in several centers during the earlier years is unlikely to have amounted in any year to more than 5 per cent of the published total for the United States.

2. While the compilation of district and national totals is made by the staff of the Board of Governors, which in cooperation with the Federal Reserve Banks edits and checks the basic data with great care, the actual collection of reports from individual banks has been

---

[9] With two minor substitutions, the reporting centers had remained the same: in 1920 Fargo, N. Dak. replaced Great Falls, Mont., and in 1928 Greenville, S. C. replaced Charleston, S. C.

[10] Thus, subsequent to January 1921, due to "a large increase in the number of reporting banks in the city of Boston," the total for this city was increased by nearly one-third. After February of the same year, the increase in the number of reporting banks in St. Louis and Louisville raised debits in these cities by about 10 and 30 per cent, respectively. Similarly after January 1922 debits in St. Paul were increased by about 20 per cent. See *Federal Reserve Bulletin* for March 1921, p. 349 and February 1922, p. 245.

With respect to Cincinnati, the *Annual Report of the Federal Reserve Board* for 1921 notes, p. 282: "Figures for 1921 are not comparable with those for preceding years owing to an increase in January 1921 in the number of reporting banks from 12 to 23." See also *Banking and Monetary Statistics*, p. 231, footnote 2.

in most cases in the hands of the local clearing house managers. In some cases reports which included debits to interbank accounts, cashiers' checks, or other items that should have been omitted, or which covered banks that should have been excluded, were furnished to the Board for many years before the errors were discovered.[11] In such cases the erroneous back data could not be corrected.

3. Numerous decisions with respect to the statistical treatment of newly chartered banks, changes in the membership of local clearing houses, bank mergers, etc., had to be made continuously by the staffs of the Board and the individual Reserve Banks. It cannot be claimed that uniform practices have prevailed over time and throughout the country. While of importance to series for individual cities, these changes had little influence on the national totals which, even after exclusion of New York, are dominated by the transactions of the large institutions in the leading financial centers. A slight upward bias, however, has undoubtedly been introduced by the merger movement to the extent that reporting institutions have absorbed banks that did not report previously.[12]

The general rule to limit debits statistics to total accounts of clearing house banks was not dropped until 1942, although beginning in the early 1920's the Federal Reserve System began to collect debits for some centers where no clearing house associations were in operation. According to a survey made by the Board of Governors, in 184 of the 274 centers for which debits were collected at that time, all commercial banks reported currently as of January 1942. In the other 90 centers there were some nonreporting banks. A survey made in 34 of these centers (including nearly all large cities) indicated that, with a few minor exceptions, the nonreporting banks were those that did not hold membership in the local clearing house association. The coverage (as measured by the percentage of deposits held by the reporting institutions) was very large even in centers where debits

---

[11] See *Banking and Monetary Statistics*, footnotes 3-18 to Table 53, pp. 246-47.

[12] See Chap. IV for a general discussion of this subject. Suburban branches are frequently established by absorption of formerly independent institutions. According to the instructions issued by the Board of Governors, debits in out-of-town branches are to be reported only if the branches are located in contiguous communities. Also, the Board's rules may not have been strictly followed and in some instances debits have probably been reported for branches that are located at some distance. It is possible that in some other cases debits at branches in contiguous communities have not been reported.

Legal provisions on branch banking vary from State to State and the growth of branch banking has been greater in some sections of the country than in others.

were reported for only a small part of the banks in operation.[13] In most cases (67 of the 90 centers), the nonreporting banks held less than 10 per cent of total deposits in their respective communities. In 17 other cases this percentage ranged up to 20 and in exceptional cases to more (in one case to more than 50 per cent).

The first major revision of the debits series was undertaken in 1942 in order to improve its coverage and to overcome the difficulties arising from the need to prorate data for split weeks so that data collected for weeks (ended on Wednesdays) could be converted to monthly aggregates. The debits series was shifted from a weekly to a monthly basis and the reporting banks began to supply deposit data comparable to the reported debits. The limitation to members of local clearing house associations was definitely abandoned, and additional banks began reporting in 21 centers where coverage had been relatively incomplete.[14] The effect of including additional reporting banks has been considerable in certain individual cities. For example, the increase has been about 55 per cent in Topeka, 14 per cent in Atlanta, and 7 per cent in Chicago. The number of reporting small centers has increased from 133 to 193.[15]

The largest change resulting from the addition of banks and reporting centers was an increase of approximately 10 per cent in the Dallas and Minneapolis district totals; the next largest change was an increase of about 8 per cent in the Atlanta District. The revision raised the New York City series by 8 per cent and the series for 140 outside centers by less than 2 per cent. Inclusion of 60 additional centers raised the reported debits of the smaller cities ("all other centers") by approximately 25 per cent above the level of the older series. In January 1951, nine additional centers were added (eight of which were in the Kansas City District) and the coverage of the national series was thus extended to 342 centers.

The series on debits to total deposit accounts, except interbank accounts, published between 1919 and 1953, covered a very large

---

[13] Only 20 of the 58 banks in New York, 10 of the 54 in Chicago, 20 of the 47 in Philadelphia, and 3 of the 14 in Atlanta reported debits in 1942. Eleven of the 18 banks in Boston and 4 of the 7 in Detroit were reporting at that time.

[14] See *Federal Reserve Bulletin*, August 1943, p. 717. For a list of these 21 centers, see the special supplement, *Revised Bank Debits Figures, May 1942-June 1943*, accompanying the Federal Reserve Board's release, *Bank Debits—Debits to Deposit Accounts Except Interbank Accounts, July 1943* (mimeographed, Aug. 11, 1943).

[15] After December 1947 the number was reduced to 192 by merger.

proportion of estimated total debits. According to estimates made by the Board of Governors of the Federal Reserve System in 1949, aggregate deposits (other than interbank) of the 333 centers which collected debits at that time covered approximately 64 per cent of estimated deposits at all commercial banks (as against 78 per cent in June 1941).

The largest coverage was in the New York Federal Reserve District (80 per cent), reflecting the very high rate of reporting in New York City where cooperating banks hold over 93 per cent of the city's deposits. In the other districts the coverage ranged in 1949 between 45 per cent (Minneapolis) and 73 per cent (Cleveland). The decline in coverage between 1941 and 1949 reflects the fact that in the intervening period business expansion had been less concentrated in the large industrial centers for which reporting coverage has always been relatively high.

DEBITS TO DEMAND DEPOSIT ACCOUNTS

When in May 1942 the older debits series was shifted from a weekly to a monthly basis, the Board of Governors began to publish a new weekly series of "debits to demand deposit accounts except interbank and United States Government accounts." These data had been collected, but not published currently, since the beginning of September 1934, when the Board of Governors had asked the weekly reporting member banks in 101 leading cities to insert in the weekly condition reports selected categories of debits for the purpose of obtaining supplementary material for research work on broad aspects of credit policy. Collection of these data was discontinued after the week ended February 1, 1939 except for the two categories "debits to demand deposit accounts of individuals, partnerships, and corporations" and "debits to demand deposit accounts of States and political subdivisions," which continued to be reported as memoranda items. The series inaugurated in 1942 represents the sum of these two items.

The continuity of the weekly series was interrupted once, at the end of July 1947, when the series of condition reports of weekly reporting member banks underwent its first major revision since its inauguration 30 years earlier. The number of reporting centers was reduced from 101 to 94, while the number of reporting member banks at the same time was increased from 371 to 441 and the percentage of total commercial bank deposits represented rose from 49 to about 57 per cent.[16] The 94 centers of the new series include 6 cities from which reports were not received previously, but whose growth since 1917 (when the series for member banks in leading cities was started) has warranted their inclusion. At the same time, 13 smaller centers were dropped from the list of weekly reporting banks. The change in the reporting group resulted in an upward shift of 19 per cent for the series for all reporting banks as judged by overlapping data for the 12 months ended June 1947; the New York series was raised by 8 per cent and that for the other leading cities by 28 per cent.

In March 1953, after considerable study of the use made inside and outside of the Federal Reserve System of the debits series then published and of their respective shortcomings, the weekly and monthly series were consolidated.[17] The series currently published, like the weekly series started in 1942, is limited to debits to demand deposit accounts except interbank and United States Government accounts.

Elimination of debits to United States Treasury accounts, including tax and loan accounts and accounts of Directors of Internal Revenue, removed from the monthly series an irregular factor not directly related to economic conditions, particularly in centers without a Federal Reserve Bank or branch but having Directors of Internal Revenue.[18]

Certain other United States Government demand accounts of a miscellaneous nature, such as those of disbursing officers, post exchanges, hospitals, etc., were not entirely eliminated. Since they are often carried in the same ledger with accounts of private depositors and might have been burdensome to segregate for reporting purposes, respondent banks were given the option of including or excluding them. The amount of such debits is very small in relation to total debits.

---

[16] See *Federal Reserve Bulletin*, June 1947, pp. 692-93.

[17] *Ibid.*, April 1953, pp. 355-57.

[18] In centers with Federal Reserve offices, Directors of Internal Revenue as a rule deposit checks directly with these offices rather than with commercial banks so that no debits at commercial banks arise when such funds are transferred to a U.S. Treasury account at a Federal Reserve Bank.

Elimination of debits to time deposit accounts had little effect on the volume of debits, since the turnover of time deposits is low and rather stable; nevertheless, it improved the significance and comparability of rates of deposit turnover. Since time deposits are rather inactive, their inclusion in the former monthly series produced differences in velocity between centers that reflected varying proportions of time and demand deposits, respectively, rather than actual divergencies in economic conditions.[19] The possibility of this result was especially great in centers where the bulk of the savings deposits was held by mutual savings banks or by savings and loan associations, which do not report debits (a few mutual savings banks were included in the reporting series prior to the 1953 revision).

Revision of the series reduced the annual figure of aggregate debits in 1952 by about 3 per cent and lowered the corresponding amounts for many centers, including New York City, by approximately the same percentage. Changes for other individual centers varied, in a few cases rather widely. The largest reductions were in cities having an office of the Director of Internal Revenue but no Federal Reserve Bank or branch, where debits representing transfers of Federal tax receipts from reporting banks to a Federal Reserve Bank were eliminated. The smallest reductions, and the few increases, were in cities in which new reporting banks or branches were added.

At the time of this revision, coverage of the series was increased to 345 centers (four added and one dropped). A number of banks were added in several centers, and the grouping of cities to obtain three breakdowns of the over-all series was changed. The publication of totals for New York City, 140 other leading centers, and 201 other reporting centers was discontinued in favor of a new three-way breakdown: New York City, 6 other financial centers (Boston,

---

[19] Longstreet and Fenn (see p. 99) found that in 1936 time deposits outside New York turned over less frequently than once a year; in New York City a slightly higher rate was due largely to the contribution of very active trust accounts classified as time deposits at three banks. The activity of time deposits ranged widely from one reporting bank to another, partly because of differences in reporting and classification practices, but district averages (excluding New York City) ranged only from 0.5 to 1.1. This velocity—confirmed by similar data available through 1939—was considerably lower than the turnover rate of 2 assumed by W. R. Burgess in the early twenties on the basis of a very small and unsatisfactory sample. It is possible, however, that time deposits were more active in the earlier period, when withdrawals could be made from savings accounts without presentation of passbooks and when there was much more leeway in the definition of a time deposit.

More recent studies conducted by the Federal Reserve Bank of Chicago suggest that savings deposits at commercial banks turn over about once every two years. See "Turnover of Midwest Savings Deposits Surveyed" and "Savings Levels and Turnover" in the Chicago Bank's *Review of Business Conditions*, March 1954 and May 1957 issues, respectively.

Philadelphia, Chicago, Detroit, Los Angeles, and San Francisco), and the remaining 338 centers.[20]

The principal value of the former series for 140 leading centers was its continuity since 1919 on a fairly comparable basis, but it included a number of relatively small centers and did not include a number of centers, now important, for which figures were not available back to 1919. The new 6-center series, consisting of the principal financial centers outside New York City and accounting for about a third of the debits outside New York City, and the new 338-center series provide more useful comparisons than the previous combinations. New York debits have accounted in each year since 1943 for more than one-third of the national total, and the other six financial centers for about an additional 20 per cent. The seven financial centers thus represent at least half of the reported debits. Monthly data for the three debits series for 1943-58 are shown in Chart II.[21]

There was no definite and logical reason for limiting the series for leading financial centers outside New York City to six cities. Additional centers, such as Cleveland or Dallas, could have been included on the basis of total volume of debits or turnover rates of demand deposits. The decision to limit the group to the six centers with the largest volume of debits to demand deposit accounts was reached mainly on the ground that the six cities represented a fairly good geographical balance, while inclusion of the three large centers following next in order of size of debits would add three Midwestern cities (Pittsburgh, Cleveland, and St. Louis).

Currently, monthly debits for each of the 344 reporting centers are published by the Board of Governors of the Federal Reserve System in a special release, "Bank Debits to Demand Deposit Accounts." This release is available 12 or 13 days after the month to which it refers and contains data by individual centers as well as subtotals by Federal Reserve districts. Dollar amounts are shown

---

[20] Beginning in April 1955, data for Paterson and Passaic, N. J. were combined, thus reducing the number of "other centers" to 337.

[21] Monthly estimates of district totals (but not figures for individual centers) on the new basis were estimated back to January 1943. Estimates for New York, 6 other financial centers, and the remaining 338 centers are also available, on a monthly basis, back to 1943. Thus for the period 1943 to February 1952, the original and the new monthly series are both available. See "Bank Debits and Rates of Turnover, Demand Deposit Accounts except Interbank and Government Accounts. Revised Series 1943-52," Board of Governors Release C.5, dated Dec. 23, 1953.

Chart 11
BANK DEBITS TO DEMAND DEPOSIT ACCOUNTS EXCEPT INTERBANK AND GOVERNMENT ACCOUNTS

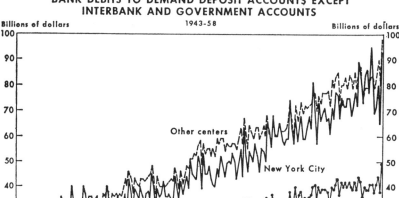

for the most recent month and three-month period of the current year and for the corresponding part of the preceding year.[22]

ESTIMATED DEBITS AT ALL COMMERCIAL BANKS

In addition to current data, the Board of Governors publishes annual estimates of debits to demand deposits and to total deposits at all commercial banks in the United States, using methods similar to those developed for the reconstruction of the historical series beyond 1919.

The first attempt to derive total debits for the entire United States, including debits at banks that did not report regularly, was

---

[22] Several Federal Reserve Banks have published, for various periods, debits for additional centers not included in the national series. Currently the Federal Reserve Bank of Minneapolis collects each month data on debits to demand deposit accounts from 247 banks not at present in the national series. The Federal Reserve Bank of Chicago also collects data on debits to demand deposit accounts for a number of banks in addition to those that are already included in the national series as well as debits against time deposits for substantially the same group of banks, and presents the data on a daily average basis rather than in terms of monthly aggregates. The Reserve Banks of Atlanta, Cleveland, Kansas City, Richmond, and San Francisco also collect debits data from a number of banks that are not at present included in the national series of reporting banks. Only the Reserve Banks of Boston, New York, and Philadelphia confine their collection of debits data entirely to the banks within their respective districts that report in the national series.

TABLE 3

SUMMARY OF DEBITS SERIES

Description	Period available	Frequency of publication	Board of Governors publication
Debits to total deposit accounts, except interbank accounts:			
New York City	Jan. 1919- Feb. 1953	Monthly[1]	*Federal Reserve Bulletin*
140 outside centers (national series)	Jan. 1919- Feb. 1953	"	"
Additional outside centers[2]	May 1942- Feb. 1953	"	"
All commercial banks	1919 to date	Annually	Annual release
Debits to demand deposit accounts, except interbank and U.S. Government accounts:			
New York City[3]	Jan. 1935- Feb. 1953	Weekly and monthly[5]	Weekly release; monthly data in *Federal Reserve Bulletin*
93 outside centers[4]	Jan. 1935- Feb. 1953	"	"
New York City	Jan. 1943 to date	Monthly	Monthly release; *Federal Reserve Bulletin*
6 other financial centers	Jan. 1943 to date	"	"
337 other centers[6]	Jan. 1943 to date	"	"
All commercial banks	1919 to date[7]	Annually	Annual release

[1] Prior to May 1942, monthly figures estimated from reported weekly totals; weekly data as well published prior to April 1927 only. Monthly data for 1919-41 are conveniently tabulated in *Banking and Monetary Statistics*.

[2] 201 centers, January 1951 through February 1953; 192 centers, December 1947 through December 1950; 193 centers, May 1942 through November 1947. A varying number of centers between 1919 and May 1942.

[3] January 1935 through June 1947 for a smaller group of banks; for the period July 1946 through June 1947, both the revised and unrevised series are available.

[4] 100 centers, January 1935 through June 1947; for the period July 1946 through June 1947, series for both the 93 and the 100 centers are available.

[5] Monthly totals estimated from reported weekly figures.

[6] Prior to April 1955, 338 centers.

[7] Prior to 1943, U.S. Government accounts are not excluded.

made by Carl Snyder, who estimated total debits at all banks in the United States by extrapolating a curve (for the single year 1922) relating cumulated debits to cumulated demand deposits at national banks in about 60 cities.[23] Morris A. Copeland later enlarged the basis for the estimate by including all of the 224 centers for which data on both demand deposits and debits were available in mid-1926.

---

[23] See "A New Index of the General Price Level from 1875," *Journal of the American Statistical Association*, June 1924, p. 190. For Snyder's estimates 1919-26, see Wesley C. Mitchell, *Business Cycles, The Problem and Its Setting*, p. 126. Subsequently, Snyder shifted the basis of estimates to 1925.

He also refined Snyder's method by estimating (1) debits to total deposits and (2) demand deposits only for five size groups of centers (classified according to size of deposits) within each of 10 separate groupings of States. The final estimate was the average of estimates derived separately on the basis of demand and of total deposits (which were in most areas very similar in amount). Copeland's estimate was also made for only one year (1926), and the ratio of estimated total debits to reported debits in 194 centers outside New York found for that year was applied to debits in 140 centers for all years since 1919; to these estimates, New York debits as reported were added.[24]

Copeland's method was subsequently somewhat modified and simplified by the staff of the Board of Governors, which grouped banks by size of community in which they were located rather than by geographic location and size of deposits. The turnover ratios for total deposits obtained—once more for a single year, 1930—were again applied to deposits at institutions not reporting debits, and total debits for all other years were estimated on the assumption that the 1930 ratios held true for all previous and subsequent years.

Similarly, an annual series of debits to demand deposit accounts except interbank accounts at all commercial banks, starting in 1919, was derived by the Board of Governors from the estimated series of debits to all accounts by subtracting estimated debits to time deposit accounts. The latter were estimated on the basis of assumed turnover ratios for time deposits.[25] No basic revision of the method of estimating these two series has been made for the past 30 years.

NEW YORK CITY DEBITS

In financial centers, and most notably in New York City, the amount of debits is strongly affected by changes in the volume of financial transactions. For this reason, "outside" debits are usually used in studies of business activity. New York debits have been used in studies of business cycles and in economic barometers to represent "speculation" rather than "business."

---

[24] Morris A. Copeland, "An Estimate of Total Volume of Debits to Individual Accounts in the United States," *Journal of the American Statistical Association*, September 1928, pp. 301-03. Copeland's estimate was 7 to 8 per cent higher than Snyder's, but the percentage difference was almost constant for all years after 1919.

[25] For details, see *Banking and Monetary Statistics*, pp. 232-33.

Financial debits are, of course, not the only factor responsible for the disproportionately large volume of New York debits. Much of the business of New York banks is of national rather than local scope. New York banks handle accounts of a long roster of the country's larger corporations, a considerable proportion of which have chosen New York as their corporate headquarters. Dividend and interest checks of these and other corporations for which New York banks act as registrars and bond trustees are drawn on New York institutions. Borrowers from other parts of the country maintain active accounts with New York banks, whose lending activities are by no means confined to the New York area.

The role of New York City as the nation's foremost wholesale center gives rise to additional debits that are related to business conditions in the country as a whole rather than in New York City alone. The concentration of corporate and wholesale activities in New York thus tends to reduce outside debits in relation to gross national product and inflates New York debits correspondingly. For that reason, the high level of debits in New York partly reflects its importance as the nation's corporate and wholesale capital in addition to its position as the financial center of the nation.

Direct analysis of the movement of debits arising from financial transactions as contrasted with debits reflecting payments related to production and distribution is not possible because information on the distribution of debits by classes of depositors or by types of transactions is not available. Indirect data are not sufficiently comprehensive for estimating the proportion of New York debits that originates in financial transactions, or more particularly in securities trading.

Historical data on some segments of the securities market, such as over-the-counter trading in Government securities and in unlisted securities, are almost entirely lacking.[26] Debits also arise from borrowing by brokers and their customers, but statistics on the amounts of securities loans extended are not available.[27] A further complica-

---

[26] For the estimated value of over-the-counter stock transactions, 1919-49, see Irwin Friend and Associates, *The Over-the-Counter Securities Markets.*

[27] The total amount of bank loans made during a given year cannot be estimated from information on the amount of loans outstanding. Turnover rates of loans of the same category vary considerably. Day loans may be repaid before the end of the business day on which they are negotiated. Call loans are day-to-day loans, but may be renewed. There is on record at least one call loan which had a life of 14 years

tion is underlined by surveys made in recent years which indicate that more than two-thirds of all transactions on the New York Stock Exchange are for persons and institutions domiciled outside New York City.[28] It is not known, of course, whether this proportion holds true in earlier years as well; moreover, some customers residing in other States still may have checking accounts with New York banks in which their transactions on the Stock Exchange would be reflected.

Finally, while data on new capital issues in the United States are available, the portion floated in New York City is not known. Moreover, data on new capital issues do not reveal the full amount of financial debits involved. The mechanics of underwriting may involve successive payments that total a multiple of the amount issued; thus the proceeds of the issues are paid in the first instance to the issuing corporations, but before the securities reach the final investor, payments arise between the underwriting group, the distributing syndicate, and retailers of securities. At the other extreme, refunding issues may represent direct exchanges with no cash payments involved.

Investigation of the contribution of financial transactions to New York debits and clearings must, therefore, draw upon subsidiary material, primarily the statistics compiled by the Stock Clearing Corporation, through which the bulk of payments arising from the trading on the New York Stock Exchange is cleared so that only net balances need to be paid in cash. Data on the total amounts of money payments cleared through the Stock Clearing Corporation and on the size of the balances actually paid cover not only round-lot trading in outstanding securities, but also other types of money payments arising from securities trading and from the flotation of new issues. Payments cleared by the Corporation, however, include only transactions between brokers and dealers and some related payments, but not those between brokers and customers.

The amount of such payments from and to customers (the "outside business") cannot be estimated from the volume of sales on

---

(James H. Rogers, "The Effect of Stock Speculation on the New York Money Market," *Quarterly Journal of Economics*, May 1926, p. 4357).

[28] For surveys covering the years 1953 to 1957, see *A Picture of the Stock Market* (New York Stock Exchange, 1958).

the Stock Exchange. A large but unknown part of such transactions does not involve any transfer of funds, since customers frequently leave the proceeds of sales with brokers, ready to be drawn upon for purchasing securities. Also, the practice of trading on margin reduces the amount of check payments far below that of customers' aggregate transactions. In 1929, for instance, the market value of round-lot stock sales on the New York Stock Exchange has been estimated at close to $63 billion. Stock clearing arrangements reduced the amount of check payments between brokers (including payments for trading in bonds and unlisted securities and for new issues) to $22.5 billion.[29] The amount of additional check payments by buyers of securities to their brokers and by brokers to sellers, however, may have been either larger or smaller than this figure.

Although payments of balances at the Stock Clearing Corporation represent only a fraction of total debits and clearings arising out of securities trading or distribution of new issues, between 1921 and 1946 they accounted for between 2 and 4 per cent of total New York City debits. In 1947-58, they were less than one per cent of debits to demand deposits. It is likely that fluctuations in the clearing balances at the Stock Clearing Corporation (and in the total amount of contracts cleared) are rather closely associated with fluctuations in the total amount of all payments traceable to securities trading in New York City. Cyclical fluctuations in the dollar volume of stock trading at the New York Stock Exchange have been much wider than those exhibited by the gross national product and by various indicators of business activity, such as the Federal Reserve index of industrial production or debits outside New York City. Similarly, both total "contracts cleared" and actual balances paid at the Stock Clearing Corporation show ups and downs which percentagewise are several times larger than those of the indexes reflecting the volume of national production, distribution, and income.

Direct evidence of the importance of stock exchange transactions in New York debits was obtained by the author through an investigation of 25 bank accounts of New York Stock Exchange

---

[29] Between 1921 and 1957 balances actually settled at the Stock Clearing Corporation fluctuated between 15 and 31 per cent of all "contracts" cleared. In the absence of such a clearing arrangement, check payments (and the resulting debits) among brokers would have been from three to seven times as large as the amounts actually paid in each year.

firms. Debits to these 25 accounts during the month of August 1946 aggregated nearly half a billion dollars, or 1.7 per cent of total New York debits in that month. The accounts included in the sample, aggregating $22 million, belonged to the most active of their kind; on the other hand, the sample accounted for only a small part of all deposits of stock exchange firms since at the end of that same month total bank deposits and cash holdings of members of the New York Stock Exchange amounted to $403 million, nearly all presumably consisting of demand deposits. At the time the first edition of this study was written, it was thought to be improbable that the average rate of turnover of all demand deposit accounts of Stock Exchange firms would approach that of the 25 chosen at random among the most active. Assuming that the average turnover rate for accounts of all such firms was only half as large, it was estimated that the volume of debits accounted for by these firms would be one-sixth of New York City debits to total deposit accounts, except interbank accounts, reported for August 1946.

A special study undertaken by the New York Clearing House Association and submitted to the United States House Committee on Banking and Currency under date of April 6, 1959, confirms and amplifies the results of the limited exploration undertaken in 1946. The 14 banks that are members of the Clearing House Association segregated for the month of February 1959 demand balances and related debits for two categories of financial firms (1) dealers in United States Government obligations, and (2) investment dealers and brokers (including investment bankers and stock brokers). During the survey month, dealers in United States Government securities accounted for about 0.1 per cent of daily average demand deposit balances, other than interbank and United States Government balances, at the Clearing House banks; investment dealers and brokers accounted for slightly more than 2 per cent.

The results of the survey can be summarized as follows: United States Government securities dealers, numbering fewer than 20, alone accounted for almost $18.8 billion, or more than 25 per cent of debits to demand deposits reported by the 14 banks. This handful of firms accounted for more debits than were reported in the aggregate for each of nine of the twelve Federal Reserve districts. Investment dealers and brokers accounted for debits aggregating close to $9.3 billion. The combined debits reported by those two categories of financial firms alone are responsible for almost 38 per cent of debits of New York Clearing House banks (debits at other reporting banks accounted for less than half of one per cent of the New York total). Had the survey been expanded to cover some minor categories of financial firms or debits arising from portfolio adjustments of life insurance companies and other financial intermediaries, or from the temporary investment of excess funds by corporations, the share of financial debits would have risen substantially above 38 per cent.

From the Clearing House survey data, turnover rates for the month of February 1959 for the two categories of financial firms can be computed. These work out to 938.7 for dealers in United States Government securities and 24.9 for investment dealers and brokers. In other words, because of the highly efficient organization of the payment and delivery mechanism in the market for United States Treasury securities, which involves a very small number of firms located within a few blocks, it is possible to make from a bank account payments averaging *each working day* 50 times the opening balance. Because of the larger number of participants in the stock market (and related underwriting, distribution of, and over-the-counter trading in private securities), turnover rates of demand deposit accounts maintained by firms in the investment dealer and broker categories do not quite reach the same high figure. However, even in this area, balances on the average turn over more than once every working day.

If the February ratios are multiplied by 12 (and seasonal influences are disregarded), yearly rates of turnover of 11,264 for Government securities dealers and 299 for all other securities brokers and dealers are obtained. All other accounts, however, turned over in February 1959 at an estimated annual rate of only 34.4 (computed by deducting the two segregated categories from debits to demand deposits other than interbank and United States Government accounts and the related average deposits reported by the 14 Clearing House banks), which is not appreciably higher than the 24 times a year for "all other reporting centers," and the 31 times in the six leading financial centers outside New York City.

The data obtained by the New York Clearing House survey fully confirm the views generally held on the influence of financial transactions on New York City debits and rates of deposit turnover. They furthermore highlight the extent to which, since the thirties, and in particular since World War II, check payments related to the issuance and refunding of, and trading in, United States Government securities have come to supplant those arising from Stock Exchange transactions as the main type of financial debits.

Between 1919 and the end of World War II, changes in New York debits (and clearings) were fairly closely associated with the volume of trading on the New York Stock Exchange and of new securities floated;[30] differences between the amplitude of cyclical fluctuations of New York and of outside debits were clearly related to the volume of securities traded. Since World War II, this relationship, while still clearly traceable, is less regular, as other types of financial payments, including those related to the frequent and large refundings of public debt, and more generally to trading in Government securities, have become a more significant factor in New York debits.

The very large gains in New York City debits during the twenties reflected chiefly financial and speculative activity; the sharp drop in such activities during the Great Depression provides the main explanation of why debits declined relatively more in New York than in the country as a whole, and why both series of debits declined appreciably more than gross national product. Financial activities in New York City failed to recover after 1933 to the same extent as production and trade in the country as a whole, thus reducing the ratio of New York debits to debits of all commercial banks.

Every time that financial and speculative transactions declined, the importance of New York City debits relative to estimated debits at all commercial banks in the United States declined markedly (see Chart III, page 45). In 1919, 37 per cent of all debits in the country (excluding interbank payments) were to accounts at reporting New York City banks. In the following year, when the volume of trading on the New York Stock Exchange contracted sharply, this percentage dropped to 33; it increased gradually during the years of the rising stock market to a high of 47 per cent in 1929 and declined thereafter

---

[30] For a more detailed discussion, see the first edition of this publication, pp. 39-42.

continuously throughout the thirties into the early war years.[31] By 1942 the percentage had declined to 26 and it reverted to this figure after the war years when it rose as a result of the concentration of war financing activities in New York. The new series of debits to demand deposits, other than interbank and United States Government accounts, shows that the share of New York City in total reported debits has been rising. The second segment of the curve on Chart III is on a higher level, since the total does not include estimates for nonreporting banks. The percentage shows the same wartime bulge as the first segment, but then rises from a low of 35.3 per cent in 1951 to 39.3 per cent in 1958.

As noted above, debits in centers other than New York also include a varying proportion of financial debits. These arise from transactions at local stock exchanges, from local flotation of securities, from portfolio adjustments, from trading in Government and unlisted securities, or from other financial transactions. Even trading on the New York Stock Exchange involves transfers of funds by out-of-town interests and by branches of New York brokerage firms located throughout the country. The same is true for dealers in Government securities, investment bankers, and other financial firms, all of whom maintain nationwide sales organizations and make use of local banking facilities. Nevertheless, with the exception of the six financial centers for which a separate debits series is being published currently and some other regional financial centers, financial transactions are small relative to commercial, industrial, and personal debits, particularly in country banks, whereas in New York the converse is true. In times of active speculation, however, the increased volume of financial transactions may be clearly traced in the debits and clearings series for most of the leading financial cities.

---

[31] Actually, the decline of New York City's share in the national total after 1929 has been even more pronounced, since beginning in 1942 the New York totals have been increased by inclusion of additional banks whose debits were not previously included with the New York City series. For instance, in 1942 debits at reporting New York banks were the same percentage of the national total as in 1941 only because of the inclusion of four additional banks in the New York reporting group; on the basis of the 1941 coverage the percentage would have declined from 26 to 24. For details, see the first edition of this pamphlet, Appendix II.

Chart III

NEW YORK DEBITS AS A PERCENTAGE OF DEBITS TO ESTIMATED TOTAL DEPOSIT ACCOUNTS AT ALL COMMERCIAL BANKS IN THE UNITED STATES, 1919-50, AND OF DEBITS TO DEMAND DEPOSIT ACCOUNTS AT ALL REPORTING BANKS 1943-58

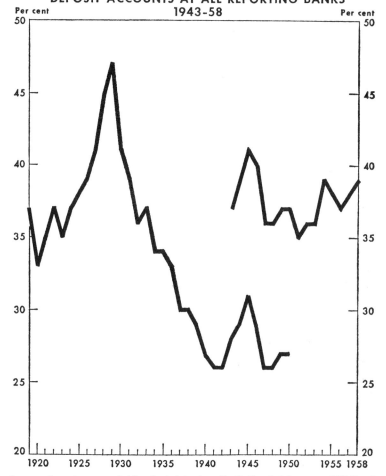

Sources.—Percentages computed from basic data released by the Board of Governors. 1919-50, estimated debits to total accounts, except interbank accounts, at all commercial banks; 1943-58, debits to demand deposit accounts, except interbank and U.S. Government accounts, at all reporting banks. New York debits for the first segment are raised from published data to include several smaller clearing house banks which were not included in the original series.

IV. Comparison of Clearings and Debits

Basically, debits are more comprehensive as a measure of aggregate money payments than clearings because they include a variety of charges arising from business activities and from personal spending that do not find their way into the clearing process. At the same time, they are more homogeneous than clearings because they relate to charges to nonbank deposit accounts only. The various items normally included in or excluded from the two statistical series are indicated in Table 4. Obviously, not all checks and drafts that may be cleared actually reach the clearing house; some (unknown) proportion of such items is presented over the counter or through the mails to the drawee banks, thus by-passing clearings.[1]

In terms of dollar volume, the main class of items included in clearings but not in debits to demand deposit or total deposit accounts is drafts on interbank accounts. This difference emerges plainly from examination of items cleared through the Federal Reserve System and the clearing houses in leading cities, as well as from such fragmentary statistics on debits to interbank accounts as are available. Drafts on interbank accounts exchanged at clearing houses include drafts on correspondent banks as well as on reserve balances at the Federal Reserve Banks and may include Federal Reserve exchange drafts.[2]

Another source of difference between clearings and debits arises from the participation of the Federal Reserve Banks and their branches in check clearings in Federal Reserve Bank and branch cities (usually as special members of the clearing association or under some similar arrangement). In many of these cities checks drawn on Treasury accounts at the Federal Reserve Banks are usually collected

---

[1] Checks exchanged at the clearing house normally include a small proportion of items that are "not good," mis-sent, or not properly signed or endorsed. Such items are returned to the sending bank. A cashier's check is usually issued to the returning bank for dishonored items. Dishonored items cleared thus do not give rise to debits, but to a double clearing, as the cashier's check is normally put through clearings. Mis-sent items and items returned for correction are usually exchanged at the next clearing and thus enter twice into clearing totals.

[2] Cashiers' and miscellaneous expense checks may be cleared, as are all other checks, although banks reporting debits are instructed to exclude them. Individual accounts are debited at the time cashiers' (or certified) checks are issued and so inclusion of both items in debits would result in double counting.

TABLE 4

COMPARISON OF ITEMS INCLUDED IN DEBITS AND CLEARINGS

Item	Drawee	Debits to		Clearings[1]
		All deposit accts. except interbank (prior to 1952)	Demand deposit accts. except interbank and U. S. Govt. (since 1943)	
Checks on demand deposits of individuals, partnership, and corporations	Com'l bank	Yes	Yes	Yes
Checks on demand deposits of States and political subdivisions	Com'l bank	Yes	Yes	Yes
Checks on U.S. Government accounts	Com'l bank	Yes	No	Yes
Withdrawals from Treasury tax and loan accounts	Com'l bank	Yes	No	No[2]
Withdrawals from savings accounts	Com'l bank	Yes	No	Yes[3]
Remittance and other bank drafts	Com'l bank	No	No	Yes
Cashiers' checks	Com'l bank	Yes[4]	Yes[4]	Yes
Charge tickets and other authorizations	Com'l bank	Yes	Yes	No
Officers' checks for salaries, expenses, and dividends	Com'l bank	No	No	Yes
Member bank drafts[5]	F. R. Bank	No	No	Yes
Federal Reserve exchange drafts	F. R. Bank	No	No	Yes
U.S. Treasury checks	F. R. Bank	No	No	Yes
Checks on foreign accts.	F. R. Bank	No	No	Yes[6]
Postal money orders	Post Office	No	No	Yes

[1] At the New York Clearing House. As each local clearing house makes its own rules, the treatment of the various items is not uniform throughout the country. The items payable at Federal Reserve offices enter local clearings only in centers where such offices are located.

[2] Except when a bank that is not a member of the Federal Reserve System and does not maintain a clearing account with the Federal Reserve Bank meets withdrawals by drawing on a clearing house bank, or when a member bank uses this means of meeting a withdrawal.

[3] Except when withdrawals are paid in cash.

[4] Except when purchased for cash.

[5] Also drafts on clearing accounts of nonmembers.

[6] In New York City only; nominal amounts also in two other cities.

through local clearings, although large checks are frequently deposited directly in order to replenish reserve balances. Similarly, Post Office money orders are generally exchanged at clearings but are not reported as debits.[3] Finally, in New York City practically all checks drawn on accounts of foreign governments or foreign central banks at the Federal Reserve Bank are included in clearings but not in debits.[4]

Debits, although restricted to charges against nonbank accounts carried by commercial banks, include several important categories of charges that do not reach local clearing houses. Among the additional charges included in debits are cash payments of checks presented over the counter or received through the mails (called "on us" checks), withdrawals of currency by depositors, payments (of notes, securities, acceptances, etc.) authorized by advices, letters, standing orders, etc., as well as for various services performed by the bank. Moreover, all telegraphic and telephonic transfers of funds by-pass clearings. Prior to the 1953 revision, an additional difference arose from the inclusion of debits to time deposits in the old monthly debits series. The exclusion of debits to United States Government accounts has removed from reported debits still another category of payments that enters clearings in appreciable proportions (payments of calls on Treasury tax and loan accounts, however, ordinarily enter neither the clearings nor demand debits series).

As clearings data are not classified by type of instrument cleared, it is impossible to estimate what proportion of checks cleared in a given city consists of items that are not included in debits statistics. Conversely, only fragmentary data are available concerning the volume of some of the separate items included in debits but not in clearings. On the basis of such evidence as is available (see pages 55ff), it appears that, in financial centers at least, the inclusion of bank drafts in clearings but not in debits is probably a major reason for differences in year-to-year fluctuations in the two series for a particular center. The bulk of clearings, however, consists of checks chargeable to individual accounts at commercial banks; consequently

---

[3] The amount of Postal money orders cleared increased significantly in all Federal Reserve cities after the change in Postal money order procedure that became effective July 1, 1951.

[4] The amount of checks drawn against foreign accounts at other Federal Reserve Banks is negligible when compared with total debits.

a very large proportion of the items exchanged at local clearing houses is included in the debits as well as the clearings series.

The relative proportion of checks presented directly to drawee banks (or their branches), thus by-passing clearings, varies from locality to locality. In general, the more the banking resources of a community are divided among independent institutions, the larger the proportion of checks against customers' accounts passing through local clearing houses. The volume of bank drafts cleared is largest in Federal Reserve Bank and branch cities; it is likely to be altogether negligible in small centers. As compared with the total volume of clearings, the total amount of items payable at the Reserve Banks and their branches in clearings (Treasury checks, Federal Reserve drafts, and Postal money orders, and in New York City items on foreign accounts) was exceedingly small prior to World War II.

RELATIONSHIP BETWEEN DEBITS TO INTERBANK ACCOUNTS AND DEBITS TO ALL OTHER DEPOSIT ACCOUNTS

Since the main difference in the coverage of the clearings and debits series is to be found in bank drafts, some light on the way clearings are affected by the inclusion of interbank payments is shed by an examination of the relationship between the two series.

Charges to interbank accounts may be classified in two groups:

1. Transactions directly related to the flow of funds in the non-banking segment of the economy. This category includes collection and clearing of commercial checks and of noncash items, purchase of securities and of foreign exchange, and transfer of funds for the account of customers (such as national corporations).

2. Transactions arising from changes in bank reserve positions or from the management of investment portfolios of banks rather than from their collection and clearing functions. This category includes transfers of funds to reserve accounts at the Federal Reserve Banks or to deposit accounts at other banks, and payments resulting from interbank borrowing and from the investment of free balances through correspondent banks. These debits to interbank accounts, although related to some extent to debits originated by depositors, are probably less closely related than the latter to the volume and timing of the flow of payments of the first category.

No numerical data on the relative importance of the two types of debits to interbank accounts are available. It is likely, however, that in clearing house exchanges the first type bulks large in comparison with the second type. Normally, all checks deposited out of town are collected through correspondent banks or the Federal Reserve System. Usually, collection of checks and of noncash items involves simultaneous use of both channels. As procedures for the handling of collections for correspondent banks vary greatly, the volume of debits to bank accounts which the collection of $1 million of checks necessitates may fluctuate from zero to several million. Differences in accounting practices, in the use of reciprocal balances, and in the routing of checks (a check routed through several banks may originate several debit and credit entries) largely explain why the ratio of debits to interbank accounts to debits to all other accounts may be large in one financial center and small in another.

The connection between debits to interbank accounts and the collection of checks and of noncash items may be summarized as follows:

1. Checks on local banks. The bulk of checks exchanged in clearing house centers results in offsets. The residual balances (which in large centers usually amount to about one-tenth or less of the total volume of exchanges) are usually adjusted on the books of Federal Reserve Banks (or their branches). Only a relatively small proportion of checks on local banks deposited in the same city gives rise to debits to interbank accounts.

2. Checks deposited out of town. Collection of checks deposited out of town may involve one or several debits to interbank accounts, although under certain arrangements no such debits arise. When checks drawn against and collected by member banks are routed directly through the Federal Reserve System, reserve balances are used as a clearing fund.[5] Banks that are not members of the Federal Reserve System usually remit for Federal Reserve cash letters by drawing on their city correspondents and a large proportion of such

---

[5] Different methods are used by the various Federal Reserve Banks for obtaining payment for out-of-town cash letters. After experimenting with charging reserve accounts for cash letters according to a fixed time schedule, the practice was adopted of charging member bank accounts upon the receipt of remittance drafts or of authorizations to charge. Some of the remittance drafts are collected through local clearings. More recently there has been a growing tendency to accept other forms of payment for cash letters, all of which by-pass clearings. A drawee bank may simply return an authorization to charge its reserve account; or it may order an out-of-town correspondent to transfer funds to the Federal Reserve Bank by wire or mail.

drafts passes through clearings in Federal Reserve and branch cities.

When checks are collected through correspondent banks rather than through the Federal Reserve System, remittance drafts on correspondent banks are forwarded unless other arrangements are made. Normally, balances with correspondent banks serve as a clearing fund and items against country banks automatically result in a corresponding debit to the account of the country bank on the books of the city bank. If a check passes through several city banks, several successive debits to interbank accounts usually result.

While, in spite of duplications, the amount of debits to interbank accounts arising from the collection of checks is probably on the whole smaller than the volume of the underlying flow of commercial funds, it is likely that fluctuations in the two magnitudes (and consequently in debits to all other accounts) are closely interrelated. Only a relatively small proportion of interbank funds, however, is transferred by bank drafts and is likely to be included in local clearings. Since correspondent relationships usually work both ways, offsetting transactions (including investment of free balances) tend to reduce transferable balances. Also, interbank balances are transferred by means other than drafts, notably through the Federal Reserve or other telegraphic wire systems.

In the comparison of debits and clearings for an individual city, account must be taken of the fact that in many cases bank drafts arising from the collection of checks (and of noncash items) are cleared in localities other than those where the checks are payable. Thus, when a country bank in Scranton remits for a cash letter by drawing on a Philadelphia bank, checks covered by the cash letter will be included in Scranton debits (but not in clearings), while the remittance will enter into Philadelphia clearings (but not debits). Conversely, when city banks collect through correspondents in smaller centers, all or part of the items may be cleared locally, but remittance drafts are likely to be cleared in some distant financial center. Thus if a Scranton bank collecting a check for its New York correspondent remits in Philadelphia funds, the draft deposited by the New York bank with its Philadelphia correspondent (or with the Federal Reserve Bank) is likely to be cleared in that city while the debit for the underlying business transaction will be reported in Scranton.

As remittances of country banks to their city correspondents or to Reserve Banks (and similarly funds transferred by city banks to build up their reserve balances or balances with country bank correspondents) are as a rule payable in financial centers, a large proportion of such drafts is likely to be cleared there. On the other hand, the underlying collection items are frequently not exchanged at a clearing house, either because they are forwarded to the drawee bank directly or because there is no local clearing house.

TECHNICAL FACTORS AFFECTING CLEARINGS AND DEBITS

Notwithstanding differences in composition, debits and clearings for the same city or for the country as a whole show very similar cyclical fluctuations, as will be shown in Chapter VI. This is not altogether surprising inasmuch as the amount of interbank transactions —which are the main additional items covered by the clearings series —is rather closely related to the volume of payments made by individuals, business establishments, and Government units. Data for individual cities, however, are in some cases subject to certain systematic biases or occasionally to sudden upward and downward shifts caused by changes in the reporting group or in operating procedures rather than changes in business and monetary conditions. Some of the common causes of these technical imperfections are important in individual localities but submerged in the aggregate series for the country as a whole.

Changes in membership of clearing house. The consistency over time of the clearings series for an individual city is automatically affected by changes in the membership of the local clearing house association and by changes in the local banking structure resulting from the chartering of new banks and bank suspensions and liquidations. Prior to May 1942, since debits were generally collected from clearing house banks only in centers where clearing houses were in operation, any change in the membership of a clearing house association usually affected the debits as well as the clearings series for the locality concerned. In general, however, all large banks in financial centers and all banks in the smaller cities have participated in local clearing arrangements from the time of their inception. In most cases, therefore, additions to membership have involved smaller institutions or newly formed banks. Withdrawals have been infrequent, except because of failure or voluntary liquidation or occasionally because of conflicts of one kind or another in local clearing house associations.

Mergers. If a merger involves a clearing house bank it always reduces local clearings but has only an indirect and practically negligible effect on debits. Mergers result in the concentration of accounts in a smaller number of banks, thus increasing the proportion of checks that are payable at the bank where they are deposited. One of the two merging banks usually becomes a branch, and its checks, when deposited with the head office or another branch, are no longer exchanged at the local clearing house; the reported clearings totals are consequently reduced. Debits for these checks, however, continue to be reported. When a member of the clearing house absorbs an institution that has not cleared previously, however, both clearings and reported debits increase, unless the bank reported debits previously or unless special adjustments are made, such as in the case of reported New York debits prior to 1952.

Growth in membership of the Federal Reserve System. Two important factors which, after World War I, tended to decrease the use of interbank balances for check clearing and collection are the growth of the Federal Reserve System and the extension of branch banking, in particular since World War II. With the gradual increase in membership and the lengthening of the par list, the amount of checks cleared through the Federal Reserve System has increased considerably. However, the hopes of the original framers of the Federal Reserve Act that the whole clearing and collection function would be concentrated in the System have not been fulfilled and many member banks have continued to collect all or part of their items through correspondent banks. Nevertheless, checks sent by country banks to their city correspondents for collection in many cases ultimately pass through the Reserve Banks. City correspondents usually collect local items through clearings, but forward many or all out-of-town items to the regional Federal Reserve Bank, its branches, or to other Federal Reserve Banks (making use of the direct sending privilege). Consequently, even though a large proportion of the collections of country banks is sent to city correspondents (thus increasing the activity of interbank balances in reserve cities), the amount of duplication and reduplication in debits to interbank accounts is less than it would be if the items were not ultimately channeled to the Reserve Banks. The ratio of clearings to debits will normally rise when the volume of checks collected through the local Federal Reserve office increases in relation to those received in cash letters from out-of-town banks.

The proportion of checks ultimately collected through the Federal Reserve Banks has been increasing continuously, as may be shown indirectly by relating the amount of checks and drafts handled by the 12 Reserve Banks to total debits to demand deposit (except interbank) accounts of all commercial banks. During 1920–22 the dollar amount of checks and drafts cleared through the Federal Reserve System equaled 25 per cent of estimated total debits to demand deposit accounts. In 1941 the percentage was nearly twice as large.[6] A special study revealed that in July 1952, nearly one out of every three checks paid by commercial banks (other than those cashed over the counter or "on us" checks deposited by customers) was received through Federal Reserve channels.

Growth of branch banking. Along with the increase in the scope of Federal Reserve collection activities (aided by the gradual and substantial reduction in availability schedules), the decline since World War I in the number of bank offices has tended to reduce the volume of clearings without affecting the amount of debits reported. Bank mergers in different localities also tend to reduce the volume of remittance drafts. The growth of branch, group, and chain banking has the same tendency.[7] The number of commercial banks was more than halved between the end of 1919 and the end of 1957, decreasing from 28,489 to 13,566, while the number of branches of commercial banks increased from 1,281 to 7,968.

---

[6] This comparison has two limitations: First, there is some duplication inasmuch as certain items are handled by more than one Federal Reserve Bank. Detailed data available prior to 1925 indicate, however, that checks handled by more than one Reserve Bank equal not more than 5 per cent of the amounts cleared, and this proportion has probably declined with the increased use of the direct sending privilege. Second, items handled by the Federal Reserve System include interbank drafts as well as commercial checks. This fact is unlikely to introduce a considerable bias unless the proportion (which is unlikely to be very large) of such drafts in the total amount cleared has changed considerably over time. While this ratio overstates the proportion of items chargeable to individual accounts that are collected through the System's facilities, its continuous and marked increase is significant.

[7] See John M. Chapman and Ray B. Westerfield, *Branch Banking, Its Historical and Theoretical Position in America and Abroad,* pp. 243-44.

Collection of items by and through branches involves internal accounting within a banking institution whereas the same routing among independent units necessitates remittance for cash letters. It is presumably for this reason that in the San Francisco District, where branch banking predominates, the ratio of interbank deposits to all other demand deposits is much lower than in the country as a whole. It is also likely that in some instances members of bank chains and groups use collection arrangements which, on balance, reduce the amount of bank drafts in circulation. It seems reasonable to assume that the considerable decline in the number of banking offices since World War I and the growth of branch banking in some parts of the country have tended to reduce the circulation of bank drafts in relation to total debits.

CLEARINGS AND DEBITS, 1920-58

What has been the combined effect of (1) bank liquidations and mergers, (2) growth of branch banking and of membership in the Federal Reserve System, (3) changes in the amount of bank drafts cleared, (4) changes in the relationship between checks (other than bank drafts) cleared and checks by-passing clearings, and (5) reporting of debits by banks not participating in clearings, and vice versa, on the relationship between debits and clearings? The answer to this question is suggested by changes in the ratio of clearings to debits for a large group of important centers (excluding, for reasons given above, New York City). These changes are shown for a period of nearly 40 years in Chart IV on the following page.[8]

The slight increase in the ratio of clearings to debits from .81 in 1920 to .85 four years later probably reflects the effort of the Federal Reserve System to expand the use of its clearing facilities. As a matter of fact, in 1924 the 12 Federal Reserve Banks handled a dollar volume of checks that was nearly 70 per cent greater than in 1921, while in the same period outside clearings increased by only 28 per cent. During the 10 years following 1924, the ratio of clearings to debits declined to .62 as a result of bank mergers, failures, and liquidations,

---

[8] Ratios are based on clearings in 142 identical centers and debits in 140 identical centers; 98 centers are common to both series. The additional centers included in one or the other series are relatively small, having accounted in each year for not more than 1 per cent of the respective series. The clearings series for 142 centers was obtained by eliminating from the series for 145 identical centers published in the *Statistical Abstract of the United States*, 1937, clearings for three centers which subsequently ceased reporting; this series was continued by the author through 1950.

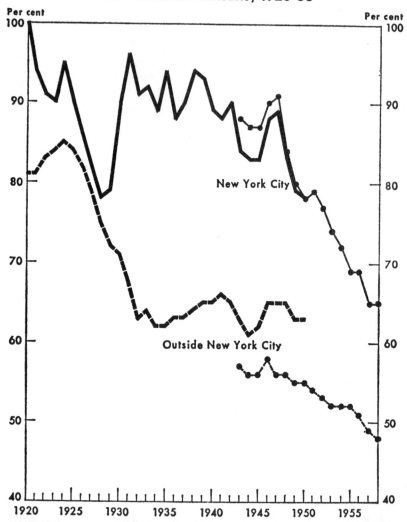

Chart IV
RATIO OF CLEARINGS TO DEBITS, NEW YORK
AND OUTSIDE CENTERS, 1920-58

Source.—Clearings, *Commercial and Financial Chronicle* and the Los Angeles Clearing House Association; debits, Board of Governors of the Federal Reserve System. The first segment of the curve for outside
centers, 1920-50, is based on clearings for 142 centers and now superseded debits series for 140 centers;
the second segment, 1943-58, is based on clearings for a variable number of centers, declining from 183
in 1943 to 176 in 1958, and debits for 343 outside centers. In the New York ratio, the new series for debits
to demand deposits has been substituted in the second segment; because it includes additional banks, the
ratio for the overlapping period is higher for the second segment.

and also because more rapid and convenient means for transferring bank funds had become available.

It is probable that the slight but regular increase from .62 to .66 in the ratio of clearings to debits in the group of identical cities outside New York between 1935 and 1941 reflects essentially the further progress made by the Federal Reserve collection system. The off-setting effect of bank mergers and liquidations, which were much less numerous in this period than during the twenties and in the depth of the depression, was apparently slight.

The outbreak of World War II caused a temporary drop in the ratio of clearings to debits. The growth of clearings lagged increasingly behind that of debits, causing the ratio of the two series to drop in 1944 to an all-time low of .61. The reason for this decline must be sought in changes in the nature and direction of money flows caused by the purchase of a large proportion of the national output by a single buyer—the Federal Government. Also, purchases of large amounts of Government securities by individuals, corporations, insurance companies, and other investors through banking institutions were recorded as debits to their accounts but usually did not involve drawing of checks that would be collected through a clearing house. Certain arrangements, such as payroll deduction plans, also tended to increase debits considerably more than clearings. Furthermore, national corporations tended to enter war bond subscriptions in localities where their manufacturing or other facilities were located. It is probable that funds shifted for this purpose gave rise to a larger volume of debits than clearings, since normally such transfers are made telegraphically.

Other wartime developments—such as the operation by many large corporations of war plants located at considerable distance from established banking connections, and the receipt of Treasury payments at one central office rather than through a widespread sales organization—probably also involved transfers of funds in such large amounts that they were more economically handled by wire than by mail. This procedure would have reduced the volume of check collection through out-of-town clearing houses. Also, the tremendously increased wartime tax revenues were credited to Treasury accounts without passing through clearing house exchanges (while the underlying tax checks were charged to individual deposit accounts), since many collectors (now directors) of internal revenue deposit tax checks directly with the Federal Reserve Banks or their branches.

Since the end of World War II, the ratio of clearings to debits has resumed its decline in New York City (where it fell from .89 in 1947 to .65 in 1957) as well as outside. Since the series for 140 outside clearings centers is not available after 1950, the chart shows, for 1943–58, the ratio of debits in all outside centers to clearings in all outside centers which report them (including Los Angeles, data for which are not carried in the *Commercial and Financial Chronicle*). The number of clearings centers declined from 183 in 1943 to 176 in 1958.

The ratio of clearings to debits in any particular city and its fluctuation over time depend largely on the importance of the given center in the country's collection system. As Table 5 shows for 1958, per capita clearings and debits also vary considerably depending on the financial importance of the reporting center.[9] On the whole, per capita debits increase only moderately with size of city. In the principal financial centers (Federal Reserve Bank cities) per capita debits are more than twice as large as in smaller cities where they include mainly local payments, such as wages, rent, and tax payments arising from the production and distribution of goods and services. A certain amount of real estate and wholesale transactions is, however, also included, particularly in cities that are centers of sizable marketing areas or wholesale markets of farm products (livestock, cotton, tobacco).

Per capita clearings show much wider variations. Because of the circulation of bank drafts and financial checks, per capita clearings in Federal Reserve and branch cities are about as large as per capita debits. In other financial centers, and in particular in the smaller cities, per capita clearings are considerably smaller than debits. In all financial centers (whether having a Federal Reserve Bank office or not) per capita debits as well as clearings are larger than in the smaller communities since they are increased by such financial ac-

---

[9] Similar relationships would be obtained for other years. For similar data for 1940, based, however, on debits to total deposit accounts, see the first edition of this pamphlet, p. 62.

TABLE 5

PER CAPITA CLEARINGS AND DEBITS TO DEMAND DEPOSITS IN 1958

[In thousands of dollars]

Reporting center or centers	Median		Range	
	Clearings	Debits	Clearings	Debits
New York City.....................	79.0	121.5		
11 other Federal Reserve Bank cities..	45.2	45.6	16.4-62.9	32.0-65.0
21 Federal Reserve branch cities[1].....	27.2	32.4	12.0-63.8	19.6-70.9
15 other financial centers[2]...........	9.1	32.4	4.1-21.7	22.3-76.7
12 selected smaller cities[3]............	2.4	13.3	1.3-11.3	7.8-21.7

[1] Including St. Paul but excluding four branch cities where no clearing house was in operation. The relatively high level of Minneapolis clearings is partly due to operations of the Twin Cities Clearing House, where Minneapolis banks exchange checks with St. Paul institutions. Items of Minneapolis banks presented there by St. Paul banks are added to Minneapolis clearings. Similarly, St. Paul clearings are increased by the amount of checks collected by Minneapolis institutions (including the Federal Reserve Bank) through the Twin Cities Clearing House. As a consequence, the ratio of clearings to debits is considerably higher in St. Paul than in centers which have no Federal Reserve Bank or branch.

[2] Where 1958 debits exceeded $5 billion: Columbus, Des Moines, Fort Worth, Hartford, Indianapolis, Milwaukee, Newark, Phoenix, Providence, Rochester, New York, Toledo, Tulsa, Washington, D.C., Wichita, and Wilmington.

[3] Aberdeen, S.D.; Elmira, N.Y.; Frederick, Md.; Holyoke, Mass.; Joplin, Mo.; Lebanon, Pa.; Lorain, Ohio; Oshkosh, Wisc.; Port Arthur, Texas; Quincy, Ill.; Vicksburg, Miss.; and Yakima, Wash.

tivities as securities trading and insurance agency transactions, and also by operations of nationwide corporations.

In 1958 per capita clearings were $79,000 in New York and more than $40,000 in each of seven other Reserve Bank cities. They were smaller but exceeded $20,000 in the four other Reserve Bank cities except Chicago, where special conditions prevailed (see page 12, footnote 16). In Federal Reserve branch cities per capita clearings ranged from less than $12,000 (Buffalo) to more than $63,000 (Jacksonville). In financial centers without a Federal Reserve Bank or branch office, they averaged only about $9,000. In the smaller cities, usually about $2,400 was cleared per capita. Per capita debits, however, ranged between $7,800 and $21,700 in these smaller cities.

While intercity differences in the absolute size of per capita debits reflect primarily the relative magnitude of financial transactions, intercity differences in the ratio of clearings to debits reflect mainly the importance of a city as a collection center. The larger the volume of interbank payments cleared, the higher this ratio. The ratio of clearings to debits is therefore generally highest in Reserve Bank and branch cities, although important regional differences arise from the uneven distribution throughout the country of nonpar banks, from which the Federal Reserve System as a rule does not collect checks. Also, the use made by member banks of the Federal Reserve collection and clearing facilities is not uniform throughout the country.

Federal Reserve Bank and branch cities, the main financial and clearing centers of the country, account for the great bulk of total clearings. In such cities, clearings are swollen by a considerable volume of bank drafts and therefore are particularly large in relation to debits.

The decline in the ratio of clearings to reported debits, in nearly all Federal Reserve and branch cities through about 1933, was a result of the trend toward greater centralization of banking resources after World War I. Largely because of mergers and consolidations in 11 Federal Reserve Bank cities (excluding New York) the number of banks reporting debits declined from 315 at the end of 1920 to 133 at the end of 1933. Similarly, the number of banks reporting debits in branch cities declined from 405 at the end of 1920 to 239 at the end of 1933. As banks reporting debits are, with relatively few exceptions, identical with those participating in local clearings, these figures also reflect the decline in the number of clearing house banks.

While many of the institutions eliminated by consolidations, failures, etc., were the smaller and weaker banks, in numerous cases leading institutions were absorbed in mergers, with the result that the proportion of checks deposited directly with or sent for collection to the drawee bank increased considerably. After 1934, the downward drift in the ratio of clearings to reported debits was arrested in most financial centers, as further consolidations became less frequent. Yet, in 1957, with one or two exceptions, clearings in all Federal Reserve office cities were a smaller proportion of debits than in 1939.

In regions where nonpar banks have been numerous, the circulation of remittance and other bank drafts has been relatively large. In 1934–38 (the only period for which such data are available) in the five districts where a large proportion of banks does not remit at par (Richmond, Atlanta, St. Louis, Minneapolis, and Dallas) debits to interbank accounts at weekly reporting member banks were equal to 50 per cent or more of debits to other demand deposit accounts; in the St. Louis District the percentage ran as high as 75 and more. In the four eastern districts in which there were no nonpar banks (Boston, Philadelphia, Cleveland—with two exceptions—and New York outside New York City), and where the Federal Reserve Banks collected items on all institutions in their respective territories, debits to interbank accounts were equal in the mid-thirties generally to less than half and frequently to as little as one-third or less of the volume of debits to all other accounts. Similar percentages prevailed in the Chicago District (outside the city of Chicago), where the number and resources of nonpar banks were relatively small, and in the San Francisco District, where nonpar banks were even less important than in the Chicago District and where branch banking was a very important factor. Owing to special conditions the Kansas City District, which includes a fairly large number of nonpar banks, showed the highest ratio among all districts of debits to interbank accounts to debits to all other demand deposits at reporting member banks. Similar differences were found in the ratios of clearings to debits in individual Federal Reserve and branch cities.

To sum up, in cities other than those in which Reserve Banks or their branches participate in local check exchanges, clearings now are usually equal to a minor and frequently declining fraction of reported debits.[10] In financial centers the dollar volume of clearings is frequently of the order of magnitude of reported debits. In some Reserve Bank cities clearings exceed total debits. This is due to a number of factors, the most important of which is the presence in clearings in Federal Reserve and branch cities of a large volume of bank drafts, reflecting collection of commercial checks drawn on other localities of the region. While the direction in which each of these various technical factors operates can be definitely established, it is generally difficult if not impossible to evaluate precisely their effect on debits or clearings for a particular city or Federal Reserve district, or for the country as a whole. Differences between the trends for clearings and debits of a particular city are usually traceable to

---

[10] In 82 such centers for which comparable figures are available, the average ratio of total clearings to reported debits was 30 per cent in 1946 as compared with 44 per cent in 1922.

differences in the degree to which technical factors affect the two series.

The discussion above is relevant to the use of clearings prior to 1919 as a substitute for debits. The case for splicing clearings to debits rests on the assumption that movements of the two series (for the same city or an identical group of centers) are closely correlated. Although overlapping data are now available for a period of 30 years, this assumption cannot be proved to be either correct or incorrect. In cities which account for the bulk of total clearings in the United States, the volume of clearings, and consequently its ratio to the volume of debits, has been considerably affected since World War I by the operations of the Federal Reserve collection system. Similarly, divergencies between clearings and debits arising from bank mergers have been a much more important consideration since World War I than in the earlier period when the total number of banks was increasing, in spite of the relatively large number of failures and consolidations. Also, the decline in the circulation of bank drafts resulting from more efficient methods for transferring interbank and reserve balances is difficult to gauge.

While the possibility of long-run drifts in the ratio of clearings to (unknown) debits before World War I cannot be minimized, they are unlikely to have been of a cyclical nature. It will be noted that in 1921 both series for outside centers showed a similar proportionate contraction and their ratio, as shown in the chart on page 56, remained the same; the sharp cyclical decline after 1929 did not interrupt the drop in the ratio that had been in evidence for several years. The smoothness of the curve shown in the chart suggests that any long-run changes in the relationship of clearings to the various categories of payments now recorded as bank debits that might have taken place prior to 1919 were probably gradual rather than abrupt. It is probable that if debits had been collected prior to World War I their cyclical fluctuations would have been very similar, at least as to timing, to the cyclical swings shown by the outside clearings series. This conclusion is reinforced by the comparative analysis of cyclical turning points in outside clearings and debits presented in Chapter VI. Its validity, however, is less certain for New York clearings (in particular with respect to amplitude of cyclical swings), mainly because of the uncertain impact of changes in the clearing arrangements for stock exchange sales and street loans.

Several investigators have either simply spliced clearings and debits in 1919, or raised the earlier series to the level of debits by multiplying it by a constant factor.[11] The general character of the change in the ratio of outside clearings and debits during the 40 years following the end of World War I, together with the high degree of conformity of turning points in the outside clearings and debits series, justifies to a certain extent the splicing of the two series for the purpose of cyclical analysis. It should be kept in mind, however, that inclusion of interbank payments in clearings may have had considerable effect on the amplitude of cyclical swings. No satisfactory method for splicing debits and clearings for the purpose of trend analysis appears feasible since our knowledge of the behavior of debits to interbank accounts is very fragmentary, and since the relationship of interbank payments to the volume of payments chargeable to nonbank accounts has been significantly affected by the operations of the Federal Reserve System.

---

[11] For an example of splicing, see Frederick R. Macaulay, *Some Theoretical Problems Suggested by the Movements of Interest Rates, Bond Yields, and Stock Prices in the United States since 1856*, and for adjustment of clearings to debits, see Carl Snyder, *Business Cycles and Business Measurements*, Chap. VI and App. Table 24.

V. Deposit Money Payments and Gross National Product

Although debits as well as clearings include payments for property transactions and various other types of business payments not arising directly from the current production of goods and services, the historical record shows that over the long pull debits and clearings have fluctuated in close relationship to gross national product (GNP). This is not surprising, since fluctuations in financial and speculative transactions are related to swings in general business conditions. Moreover, since both GNP and the series on the use of deposit money are expressed in current dollars, changes in the general price level tend to affect both series to roughly the same degree. The fact that gross national product and debits (and clearings) move together is perhaps the main reason for the continuing analytical interest in debits statistics.

WHY DEBITS AND CLEARINGS EXCEED GNP

The volume of check payments made in connection with the production and distribution of a given national product is several times larger than the dollar value of the end products. Between the two world wars, for instance, estimated total debits of all commercial banks outside New York City were in each year about six times larger than GNP, which measures the value of the total output of goods and services at the final stage (but which also includes some imputed items for which no money payments are made, at least not in the final stage).

The large size of debits and clearings in relation to GNP is not difficult to explain. Morris Copeland has distinguished between two main types of money payments:[1]

1. Transactions of the "main money circuit," which cover the bulk of payments made in producing and distributing the year's output of goods and services. Copeland's "main money circuit" transactions are, however, not identical with those arising from current production. Some transactions asso-

---

[1] *A Study of Money Flows in the United States*, National Bureau of Economic Research, 1952.

ciated with GNP are made in kind or give rise to bookkeeping entries only, while certain changes in cash balances and indebtedness are included in the main circuit.

2. Technical transactions of three kinds:

(a) Money-changer transactions—exchange of one form of money for another (check for currency, check for foreign exchange, etc.) and transfers between bank accounts.

(b) Agency transactions—payments made to or received from an intermediary which represent a single economic transaction but involve two (or more) bookkeeping entries (debits).

(c) Financial turnover transactions—offsetting portfolio investments and liquidations, new borrowing, and repayment of indebtedness to the extent that they offset each other.

Check payments for final products and payments to the factors of production alone add up to roughly twice the value of the GNP, even though some payments are made in currency. In addition, several intermediate transactions usually take place as raw materials pass through the successive stages of manufacture and distribution. The aggregate amount of payments by check before a product reaches the ultimate consumer depends on the number of intermediate transactions and on methods of payment. In general, the total amount of check payments arising in the process of production and distribution is a multiple of the value of the finished product. Thus, we may expect debits related to the production and distribution of goods and services to be a multiple of the annual value of GNP.

In addition to "main money circuit" payments, clearings as well as debits include a certain amount of payments classified by Copeland as money-changer, agency, and financial turnover transactions. Transfers of property and other assets normally involve check payments and are therefore reflected in aggregate debits. Speculative transactions, particularly in securities, represent the most important type of transactions which tends to raise the volume of both clearings and debits far above the volume of check payments arising from productive and distributive activities. Hence the attempts by various investigators to eliminate the speculative element from the time series for debits and clearings.

Speculation in securities is only one of numerous categories of transactions in property rights.[2] Several other types of transactions fluctuate either in direct or in inverse relation to the volume of business activity or are subject to autonomous, or even erratic movements. Although paucity of relevant data precludes any direct estimation of the volume of check payments arising from such transactions or of their share in clearings or debits, at different times speculation in urban or rural real estate, in various commodities, and in securities that are not traded on organized exchanges have assumed large proportions.[3] In addition to GNP-type and property payments, considerable movements of corporate and other funds take place between the various localities in which nationwide organizations maintain manufacturing operations or sales organizations. Also, numerous depositors, including Government units, maintain separate special-purpose accounts, and shifts of funds among such accounts, at the same depositary or between different institutions, are recorded as debits.

What is the share of these "technical transactions" in reported debits? Among the by-products of Copeland's work on money flows between various sectors of the national economy are estimates of debits originating in technical transactions in selected years. This so-called "fluff" represents a substantial portion of all reported debits: for the period 1936–42 as a whole, it amounted to about as much as main money circuit transactions. The relative size of technical transactions declined continuously during the seven-year period. Indeed, Copeland estimated that in 1936 technical transactions exceeded transactions in the main money circuit by about 25 per cent,

---

[2] In the last decades of the past century the volume of money payments arising from trading, including futures contracts, in farm and other products on leading commodity exchanges was so large that it was thought necessary to find a way of offsetting some of the payments. To shorten the chain of payments arising from trading in futures contracts in standard commodities, the various commodity exchanges adopted numerous types of compensating devices. In 1884 the Chicago Board of Trade formed a clearing house for the compensation of contracts and payments. A similar arrangement was begun at the New York Produce Exchange as early as 1879, but it was not until 1888 that the technique was sufficiently perfected to secure considerable economies in the amount of checks that changed hands. The Minneapolis Chamber of Commerce followed in 1891, and the New York Cotton Exchange in 1896. (See Henry Crosby Emery, *Speculation on the Stock and Produce Exchanges of the United States*, Columbia University Studies in History, Economics, and Public Law, No. 18.) Similar clearing houses for offsetting payments resulting from commodity speculation were also established at some less important futures markets.

The establishment of special organizations for the specific purpose of reducing the amount of check payments arising from commodity trading (and in particular from the speculative trading in futures) has obviously tended to minimize the inflating influence of commodity speculation on reported bank clearings and debits. In some cases, clearings were further reduced by the provision that checks in settlement of balances should be payable at a single bank acting as an agent for the commodity clearing house.

[3] The estimated value of futures trading on the commodity markets in fiscal years 1946 to 1950 fluctuated between $16.8 and $49.4 billion. See the following publications of the U.S. Department of Agriculture: Commodity Exchange Authority, *Futures Trading under the Commodity Exchange Act, 1946-54*, December 1954, p. 6; *Commodity Futures Statistics, July 1955-June 1956*, Statistical Bulletin No. 196, p. 5; and *Commodity Futures Statistics, July 1956-June 1957*, Statistical Bulletin No. 221, p. 5.

while in 1942 they were perhaps 20 per cent less than transactions in the main circuit.

The fluff was about evenly divided between New York City and outside debits to total deposit accounts, excluding interbank accounts. On the basis of income payments and related data, it may be estimated that roughly 7 per cent of GNP originates in New York City. By applying this percentage to Copeland's estimate of transactions in the main money circuit, it is possible to obtain annual estimates of the fluff for New York debits alone. The fluff in New York debits appears to have exceeded money circuit transactions nearly ten times in 1936 and nearly six times in 1942 (declining between these two years gradually from 981 to 586 per cent of main money circuit transactions). In outside debits, the fluff was considerably smaller, only about half as large as main circuit transactions; it also declined gradually from 1936 to 1942 (from 63 to 45 per cent). These rough estimates confirm once again the widely held view that New York debits represent essentially financial transactions.

For the postwar years, annual estimates of total volume of non-financial payments are available from the Federal Reserve Board's flow-of-funds project. These estimates (significantly different in concept and details from those developed by Copeland) measure in essence the volume of gross transactions between broadly defined segments of the economy that give rise to money payments. Total estimated debits after World War II remained almost twice as large as the estimated aggregate of gross nonfinancial payments in the economy, even after elimination of debits to United States Government and time deposit accounts.[4]

CORRELATION OF DEPOSIT MONEY PAYMENTS WITH GNP

In spite of all the limitations and shortcomings of the clearings and debits series discussed in the preceding chapter, these series reflect rather faithfully cyclical swings in general business conditions.

Clearings. During the period 1874-1913, for which clearings constitute the only available measurement of the volume of aggregate payments, the unadjusted series of aggregate outside clearings rose at

---

[4] In 1946, a nonfinancial flow of funds estimated at less than $750 billion compared with debits close to $1.4 trillion; in 1953, the respective figures were nearly $1,300 billion and nearly $2.4 trillion. See Board of Governors of the Federal Reserve System, *Flow of Funds in the United States, 1939-1953*, p. 390.

a rate about twice that of the GNP, as shown in Table 6. While during the first years after the end of the Civil War aggregate outside clearings were probably only slightly larger than GNP, if at all, during the last decade before World War I they were more than twice as large. During the decade 1884-93, the GNP was 33 per cent larger than during the preceding decade, and in the following two decades it grew by 32 and 83 per cent, respectively. The increase of outside clearings was much greater, notably in the earlier decades.

TABLE 6

GROSS NATIONAL PRODUCT AND OUTSIDE CLEARINGS, 1874-1913

[Dollar figures are annual averages, in millions]

Decade	GNP[1]	Outside clearings		Percentage change from preceding decade	
		Commercial and Financial Chronicle series	Macaulay's series	GNP	Aggregate outside clearings
1874-83.........	$ 8,924	[2]$11,138	[2]$12,833	....	....
1884-93.........	11,882	19,313	21,078	+33	+73
1894-1903.......	15,709	30,913	31,965	+32	+60
1904-13.........	28,783	60,585	61,602	+83	+96

[1] No annual series of GNP is available prior to 1919. Data shown are annual averages computed from decennial figures. See S. Kuznets, *National Product since 1869*, National Bureau of Economic Research, 1946, Table II, p. 119.

[2] Nine-year average, 1875-83.

Between 1875 and 1913 the annual increase of outside clearings averaged 5.7 per cent. It exceeded the rate of growth of the GNP partly because of the gradual increase in the scope of the statistical series.[5] Also, as the United States developed from a largely agricultural to a highly industrialized and diversified economy, the relative importance of market transactions involving money payments increased with the decline in the relative importance of payments in kind rather than in cash. At the same time, payment by check instead

[5] Macaulay's series, which makes an adjustment for the increase in coverage, shows an average annual increase of only 5.1 per cent.

of currency made rapid progress, particularly after establishment of the national banking system.

Interpretation of a comparison of clearings with GNP over a long period is limited by lack of knowledge concerning the effect of urbanization and the growth of the corporate form of business on the proportion of check-book money payments that is channeled through clearing houses. Did clearings represent a larger proportion of all checks in 1904-13 than in 1874-83? And did the proportion of property transactions and other payments not directly associated with the current production of goods and services increase or decrease after the early seventies? No definite answers can be given, and plausible reasons may be cited to support affirmative as well as negative answers to both questions. But in spite of these limitations, the comparison of outside clearings with GNP suggests that the production of $100 worth of goods and services required a considerably larger volume of total check payments in the last decade before World War I than it did 40 years earlier, although certainly not almost twice as many. In any case, little justification can be found for using the trend in outside clearings—as did Snyder—to represent the growth of the national economy as a whole.

While before World War I clearings increased much more rapidly than GNP, year-to-year changes in the two series were closely correlated. This is shown in Chart V on page 70, where aggregate outside clearings are plotted against Martin's estimates of "realized national income," the only comprehensive annual estimates on the total output of goods and services available for the earlier years of the clearings series.[6] This scatter diagram shows a high degree of correlation, confirmed by a coefficient of correlation of $+.997$ (for the years 1879, 1889, and 1899-1914).

In only two years between 1899 and 1915 did outside clearings deviate by more than 4 per cent from the amount expected on the basis of their long-run relationship to realized national income as expressed by the regression line. During the war years 1916-18, however, clearings increased sharply and were higher than expected values. This sharp increase in outside clearings reflected primarily the participation of Federal Reserve Banks in local clearings, which

---

[6] Robt. F. Martin, *National Income in the United States, 1799-1938*, pp. 6-7.

Chart V

BANK CLEARINGS OUTSIDE NEW YORK CITY
AND REALIZED NATIONAL INCOME
1879-1918

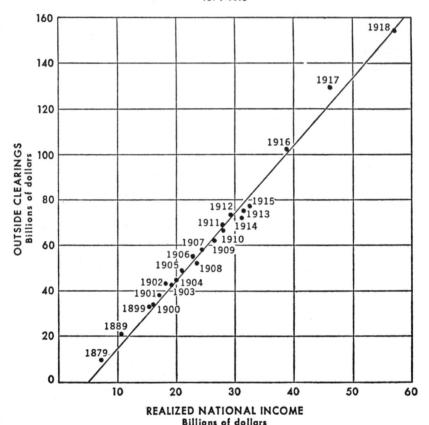

REALIZED NATIONAL INCOME
Billions of dollars

Sources.—Outside clearings: Compiled by Federal Reserve Bank of New York from the *Commercial and Financial Chronicle.* Realized national income: Robt. F. Martin, *National Income in the United States, 1799-1938,* pp. 6-7.

in some cities began as early as 1914. Presumably for the same reason, clearings continued to expand even after the armistice and failed to reflect the decline of aggregate economic activity after World War I.

As more fully discussed in Chapter II, clearings have been superseded by debits since the end of World War I, and little analytical use has been made of these data subsequent to the inauguration of the debits series. In the period for which both series are available, changes in outside clearings, as shown in Table 7, reflected cyclical changes in GNP nearly as closely as did debits.

TABLE 7

PERCENTAGE CHANGES IN GROSS NATIONAL PRODUCT, DEBITS, AND CLEARINGS, SELECTED PERIODS[1]

[Based on annual totals]

Period	GNP[2]		Debits outside New York City[3]	Clearings outside New York City[4]	Debits, New York City[5]
	Total	Non-Federal			
1919–20	+12	([6])	+14	+14	0
1920–21	−18	([6])	−21	−21	−14
1921–29	+41	([6])	+73	+54	+191
1929–33	−46	−48	−57	−64	−72
1933–37	+62	+59	+63	+73	[7]+29
1937–38	−6	−7	−13	−13	[7]−20
1938–45	+151	+74	+134	+128	+129
1945–46	−2	+36	+13	+15	+6
1946–48	+23	+26	+11	+26	+9
1948–49	−1	−2	−3	−5	+1
1949–53	+42	+30	+48	+39	+42
1953–54	−1	+3	+2	+2	+17
1954–57	+21	+24	+28	+21	+20
1957–58	−1	−1	+1	−1	+8

[1] Relatively minor contractions in 1924 and 1927 have been omitted; all three annual debits series continued to expand through the entire period 1921-29. Except where otherwise noted, basic data are from the Board of Governors of the Federal Reserve System, *Banking and Monetary Statistics*, pp. 236-37 and 254, and from the *Federal Reserve Bulletin*.

[2] Based on Department of Commerce series estimated back to 1919 by Mary S. Painter in *Federal Reserve Bulletin*, September 1945, p. 873. The Painter estimates are adjusted to revised Commerce concept.

[3] Debits to total deposit accounts in 140 centers prior to 1945; debits to demand deposit accounts, except interbank and Government, in 343 centers since 1945.

[4] 142 identical centers, 1920-49; all centers reported in the *Chronicle* plus Los Angeles clearings for 1919-20 and subsequent to 1949-53.

[5] Debits to total deposit accounts, except interbank, 1919-45; debits to demand deposits, except interbank and U.S. Government accounts, since 1945.

[6] Data not available.

[7] New York debits (revised to include debits at banks that were not included in the published series prior to 1942) reached a peak a year earlier than the series for 140 other centers and for the country as a whole. The increase is therefore measured for 1933 to 1936 and the following decrease from 1936 to 1938.

Debits. Although conceptually debits are more directly related to aggregate money payments than are clearings, this relationship has been considerably modified over extensive periods owing to special circumstances, such as the extensive speculation of the late twenties and the distortions introduced by World War II.

Prior to World War II, the outside debits series responded somewhat more strongly to cyclical fluctuations than GNP, as may be seen in Table 7. After the economic recovery that followed the armistice in 1918, debits at all commercial banks outside New York City expanded somewhat more than GNP. During the short but severe depression of 1921, debits outside New York City declined percentagewise a little more than GNP. From 1921 to 1929 outside debits increased almost without interruption and considerably more percentagewise than GNP. During the depression of the thirties, outside debits declined more than GNP (57 per cent against 46 per cent). During the recovery from 1933 to 1937 debits outside New York City rose slightly more than GNP. Again in 1938 outside debits contracted more than GNP.

During the wartime expansion in economic activity, which by 1945 brought the GNP to a level more than two and a half times that of 1938, debits outside New York City increased at a somewhat slower rate. During the entire period of World War II, the close relationship between movements in GNP and debits was disturbed by changes in the composition of the final products of the economy, in the flow of materials and intermediate products, and in the flow of payments for goods and services. An unusually large proportion of GNP was absorbed by the Government and rigid control of the flow of most materials in order to expedite production, to reduce inventories, and for other reasons, reduced the volume of inter-mediate transactions. The emergence of one large customer, the United States Government (which in the last war years absorbed nearly half of GNP), resulted in the elimination of a large number of intermediaries. The relatively large volume of goods and services purchased by the Government directly from producers kept debits below the level they would have attained if a GNP of identical size had been produced under peacetime conditions. Even though the Government's share in the total output of final goods and services was paid for with Treasury checks (which, it is recalled, are not covered by debits statistics), corresponding debits to individual accounts occurred when the funds to meet such payments were raised by the Treasury through taxation or borrowing.[7] Thus most Government expenditures for war purposes were indirectly reflected in the debits figures.

There was also a significant shift in the composition of goods

---

[7] With the exception of the relatively small amount of Federal taxes and U.S. Government securities paid for in currency. No debits to individual accounts arise, however, in the case of direct bank purchases of securities from the Treasury; only limited offerings of new issues were made to the banks after October 1943.

72

and services purchased by consumers. Purchases of consumer durable goods were proportionately smaller in comparison with expenditures for nondurable goods and services. A larger proportion of nondurable goods and of services is customarily paid for in currency rather than by check. Price fixing, the closing of many commodity exchanges, and a reduced volume of stock exchange trading are additional explanations why the increase in debits between 1941 and 1945 was less percentagewise than the rise in GNP. To a certain extent, the relative increase in cash transactions because of black market activities and tax evasion also accounts for the fact that debits grew less rapidly than GNP during the war.

While purchase of a large portion of GNP by the Federal Government tended to reduce debits, a technique for smoothing the effect of Treasury financing operations on the money market, originally evolved during World War I and generally applied during World War II, had the opposite effect. It resulted in double counting of debits arising from sales of new Government securities to nonbank investors through commercial banks. Proceeds of such sales were credited to special war loan accounts at commercial banks, with corresponding debits to the investors' accounts. A second round of debits was recorded when such funds were ultimately transferred to Treasury accounts at the Federal Reserve Banks. This inclusion of the transfer from commercial banks to the Federal Reserve Banks of the proceeds of sales of Government securities resulted in a considerable inflation of reported debits to total deposit accounts except interbank accounts (but *not* of the weekly series which *excluded* debits to United States Government accounts).[8]

From 1929 on it is possible to compare changes in outside debits with those in GNP from which Federal expenditures for goods and services are excluded. Differences in changes in total and non-Federal GNP were rather small in the three periods between 1929 and 1938, as can be seen from the first two columns in Table 7, but they were considerable during and after the war. Between 1938 and 1945, outside debits increased less than GNP, but more than GNP reduced

---

[8] During the five years 1942-46 withdrawals from war loan accounts alone aggregated $165 billion, including nearly $60 billion at New York banks reporting debits (or 3.2 per cent of New York debits during this period). No estimates of total debits (or credits) to war loan accounts at commercial banks during World War I and the subsequent liquidation period are available.

by the full amount of Federal Government expenditures for goods and services. When GNP declined slightly, as between 1945 and 1946, debits increased (reflecting the shift away from defense production), but somewhat less than GNP minus Federal Government expenditures. Thus in the defense, war, and reconversion periods, percentage changes in outside debits fell somewhere between percentage changes in total GNP and in GNP excluding Federal Government purchases, since these purchases were also reflected in debits, but on a somewhat smaller scale.

The distortions arising from the inclusion of withdrawals from tax and loan accounts (the use of which was gradually widened after the war, notably by the inclusion of withheld income and old age insurance taxes) are eliminated from the new debits series. On the other hand, Federal Government expenditures, including defense expenditures, have remained a fairly large proportion of GNP while many of the transient circumstances which distorted the relationship between debits and the value of the total output of goods and services during wartime have disappeared. Thus, the relationship between the new series of debits to demand deposit accounts (which it is recalled, was reconstructed back to 1943) and total GNP since the end of World War II has been again very close, as Chart VI shows.[9] The only exception of consequence occurred during the Korean conflict from 1951 through 1953, when Government spending rose relative to civilian expenditures. As a result, debits rose less in relation to GNP than might have been expected on the basis of the long-run relationship.

Indeed, a scatter diagram showing outside debits and private GNP alone would show a closer correlation than the relationship shown in the chart. On the whole, however, the ratio of Federal Government expenditures to total GNP has been sufficiently stable since 1947 to pose little difficulty in the use of debits to demand deposits, except Government and interbank accounts, for forecasting GNP for current periods.[10]

---

[9] For a similar chart for 1919-41 and 1946-50 based on the old monthly debits series, see the first edition of this booklet, p. 80.

[10] On the basis of data used in the chart on p. 75, it appears that for each dollar increase in GNP, the volume of debits to demand deposits other than interbank and U.S. Government accounts outside New York City increases $2.7.

Chart VI

GROSS NATIONAL PRODUCT AND BANK DEBITS
OUTSIDE NEW YORK AND SIX OTHER FINANCIAL CENTERS
1943-58

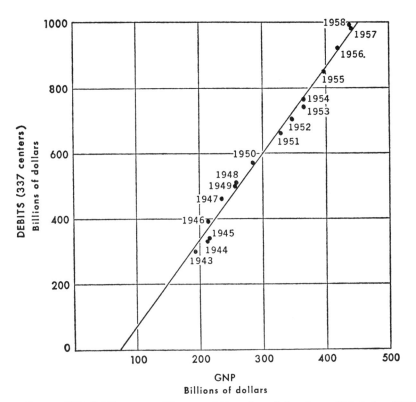

Sources.—GNP: U.S. Department of Commerce; debits to demands deposit, except interbank and U.S. Government, Board of Governors.

Since the end of World War II, with the exception of the immediate postwar years, the new outside debits series shows the same type of relationship to cyclical swings in the GNP as was observed for the old debits series during the interwar period. Again, cyclical changes in outside clearings were fairly close to those in the corresponding debits series. Debits in New York City rose considerably even in the three postwar periods of recession.

75

SUMMARY

Thus, even though the relationship between debits and GNP is by no means direct, on an annual and even on a quarterly basis the correlation between outside debits and GNP is close. In spite of the presence of several factors of change, some of which are of temporary and others of more lasting importance, the correlation between GNP and the series on the volume of deposit money transactions has been surprisingly high. Apparently the number of times each dollar of final GNP is recorded as a debit to deposit accounts of business firms and individuals is subject to long-run changes, but does not fluctuate significantly with general business conditions. On the other hand, the volume of financial and speculative transactions fluctuates on the whole with the business cycle. As a result, debits as well as clearings tend to reflect rather adequately the underlying changes in general business conditions. Furthermore, the monthly debits series for 337 "other" centers can be used with success to project current levels of GNP.

VI. Seasonal and Cyclical Fluctuations

No single category of economic time series has found such a wide and varied field of application as statistics on the volume of bank money transactions. Was the reliance placed on clearings in historical business cycle research justified by the sensitivity of the clearings data to changes in economic conditions? Are currently available debits statistics closely enough related to economic fluctuations to be of great use in current economic analysis? These and similar questions can be answered only by analyzing the extent to which the two series on bank money payments conform to the chronology of cyclical fluctuations in the American economy; this will be done in the second part of this chapter, following a section devoted to seasonal variations of the two series. For years between 1875 and the end of World War I, attention is necessarily focused on the clearings series. For the years following World War I, however, the main concern is with the debits series. For reasons stated elsewhere in this study, attention will be focused on, but not confined to, the series covering localities outside New York.

SEASONAL FLUCTUATIONS IN CLEARINGS AND DEBITS

Seasonal patterns of money payments are composites of numerous specific payment patterns. The flow of some types of payments, such as payrolls, is rather even over the year. Other important types of payments (such as taxes, dividends, or interest) are due on specific quarterly, semiannual, or even annual dates. Retail trade has its traditional Christmas and Easter shopping seasons.

The relative importance of these various types of payments has been changing over time. Moreover, the use of checking accounts for some types of transactions has been increasing. For example, the growth of charge and instalment sales has stimulated the use of checks in retail trade. The heavier tax burdens, and in particular the increased importance of the Federal individual income tax, have caused changes in the size and time patterns of check payment flows. Important but less obvious changes have been taking place in flows of business funds. The changing seasonal patterns of clearings and debits reflect the combined effects of all these changes on the aggregate amount of deposit money payments.

Seasonal fluctuations of bank clearings and debits reflect the economic structure and hence the payment patterns of the area to which they appertain. In individual cities, particularly in the smaller agricultural communities, seasonal fluctuations of debits are much more pronounced than they are in larger centers where the economic categories of payments entering into debits are more varied. When debits for a number of centers are aggregated, patterns peculiar to individual cities tend to cancel out and the seasonal patterns have a narrower range for the aggregate than for its components. For the country as a whole, the seasonal fluctuations of debits and clearings show a relatively narrow range.

The widest seasonal swings in debits are found in agricultural centers, where marketing of the main cash crops causes a sharp seasonal peak. In such cities, debits are in many cases twice as large during the months in which crop auctions are held as they are during any other month of the year.[1] This is true not only of individual agricultural centers, but also of larger agricultural areas. Thus during the twenties the seasonal index of monthly debits in the State of North Dakota reached a peak of 130 in October and a low of 75 in February.[2] In industrial and commercial centers debits fluctuate within a much narrower range, the peak month being rarely more than 15 per cent above the annual average.[3]

In the larger cities throughout the country, seasonal fluctuations are usually relatively small and reasonably uniform, reflecting in a rather similar manner the quarterly and year-end payment dates, tax payment schedules, the Christmas shopping season, and the summer vacation lull. For large geographic areas with diversified industry and agriculture, specific seasonal patterns tend to offset each other

---

[1] For instance, in Wilson, N. C., Danville, Va., and Kinston, N. C. See Federal Reserve Bank of Richmond *Monthly Review of Financial and Business Conditions*, Dec. 31, 1947, for a set of suggestive charts.

[2] Seasonal indexes for a large number of cities and for nearly all States (based on the debits for centers located in their territory) have been computed for the period 1919-30. See Standard Statistics Co., *Standard Statistical Bulletin Base Book*, January 1932, pp. 178-218. Maryland had the narrowest range of seasonal variations (95 to 109). Among individual cities, Dayton, Ohio, and Atchison, Kans., had the narrowest (in both cases 91 to 106) and Helena, Ark. the widest (70 to 161) range of seasonal variations.

[3] The same applies to clearings. For an analysis of clearings in 18 large cities, see Edwin Frickey, "A Statistical Study of Bank Clearings, 1875-1914," *Review of Economic Statistics*, August 1930, pp. 112-38.

to some extent. Thus, seasonal patterns for debits for individual Federal Reserve districts are, on the whole, rather similar. They show four peaks for months during which quarterly payments are usually made, with the fall high in October rather than September (presumably because of the crop movement), and the other peaks in March, June, and December. In Kansas City and Minneapolis, two predominantly agricultural districts, the seasonal factors are even higher for October than for December, which in all other districts is the month with the highest seasonal factor. In the industrial districts of Cleveland and Philadelphia the seasonal factors are considerably higher for December than for October. On the whole, however, the range of seasonal factors is rather small for all districts, the maximum spread being (with the exceptions of the largely agricultural districts of Atlanta, Dallas, and Minneapolis) less than 25 percentage points.[4]

Seasonal patterns of money payments have changed considerably over time. The Federal Reserve Bank of New York used a moving seasonal for outside clearings (see Table 8 below) while the National Bureau of Economic Research found it necessary to derive seasonal factors of seven separate segments between 1875 and 1942. For New York City clearings covering nearly a century, the National

TABLE 8

SEASONAL ADJUSTMENT FACTORS FOR OUTSIDE CLEARINGS AND DEBITS[1]

Month	Clearings (1875–1919)	Debits to total deposits (1919–40)	Debits to demand deposits (1943–57)
January.................	106–105	104.0–102.5	103.0–102.5
February................	97	98.0– 96.5	90.0– 91.5
March..................	97–102	99.0	105.0–106.0
April..................	101	98.5	97.0– 98.0
May....................	98	98.5	97.5– 98.0
June...................	99	100.5	101.5–102.0
July...................	96	98.5– 99.5	98.0
August.................	90	89.5– 90.5	95.0– 97.5
September..............	95	98.0	97.0
October................	107	102.0–101.0	102.5–102.0
November..............	108–106	105.0	100.0– 98.5
December..............	106–104	108.5–110.5	113.5–109.0

[1] Computed by the Federal Reserve Bank of New York. Changing factors for the months for which ranges are given (with one exception, the factors gradually increasing or decreasing within the ranges indicated); constant factors for the other months.

---

[4] This discussion is based on the seasonal patterns for individual districts for the years 1920-28 charted in B. H. Beckhart and James G. Smith, *The New York Money Market*, Vol. II, p. 267. Similar patterns based on 1919-January 1927 for the 12 districts (for the New York District, centers outside New York City only) are shown in Ada A. Matthews and A. Ross Eckler, "Regional Business Conditions: A Study of Bank Debits," *Review of Economic Statistics*, August 1928, pp. 140-55, Charts 1 and 9.

Bureau of Economic Research derived seasonal patterns for not less than 10 different successive periods. Over this longer time interval changes in the respective importance of individual months were even more substantial for New York than for outside clearings; for example, the December factor increased from 92 in 1855-67 to 115 in 1935-42.

For the period between the two world wars, the seasonal pattern for outside debits computed by the Federal Reserve Bank of New York (moving factors, 1919-40) shows June and October through December to be the months in which debits attain seasonal peaks; roughly the same pattern was found by Beckhart and Smith for individual districts in the twenties. The seasonal factors for January are also high, as some of the checks for payments due at the end of the year are undoubtedly debited after the year-end.[5] The seasonal patterns of outside clearings are very similar to those of debits for this postwar period. Seasonal factors for New York City debits have a pattern similar to that of outside debits but of somewhat larger amplitude.

The seasonal factors for the new series of debits to demand deposits in the "other" outside centers are also shown in Table 8. They have been relatively stable for the entire period 1943-57, but their pattern shows some substantial differences from the interwar pattern for the old series (notably for February, March, and November).

These seasonal adjustment factors, however, do not meet adequately the problems arising from the spread of Saturday closings and from other changing factors, and work is currently in progress to develop a better technique of adjusting debits for seasonal influences and other systematic changes.[6]

CYCLICAL BEHAVIOR OF CLEARINGS AND DEBITS

The chronology of business cycles in the United States represents one of the few areas of economic analysis in which there is a high

---

[5] In addition to the usual difficulties encountered in deriving seasonal patterns for debits, special problems were encountered prior to May 1942 when compiling monthly totals from the original weekly reports. The prorating of weekly debits between two successive months involved, among other difficulties, estimating the interweekly fluctuations of debits, the effect of the coincidence of Sundays and holidays with dates on which large payments were normally due, and the effect of holidays observed in some parts of the country but not in others.

[6] Along the lines suggested by H. Eisenpress, "Regression Techniques Applied to Seasonal Corrections and Adjustments for Calendar Shifts," *Journal of the American Statistical Association*, December 1956.

degree of agreement among the various investigators.[7] The conformity of the cyclical movements of the clearings and debits series with the generally recognized chronology of cyclical peaks and troughs has been striking.

The period 1878-1914.[8] During the period 1878-1914 the outside clearings series compiled from the *Commercial and Financial Chronicle* data expanded during each of the 10 periods of business expansion established by the National Bureau of Economic Research and declined during each of the corresponding periods of contraction (with the possible exception of the mild contraction ended in January 1912). The cyclical expansions and contractions, while clearly marked, were superimposed on a strong upward trend reflecting the increase in the volume of check-money payments as well as the general increase in the number of reporting centers.

Indeed, for the last business cycle before World War I, average daily clearings amounted to $202 million, more than six times greater than in the first full cycle covered by the data (1878-85).[9] Because of the underlying trend, the pattern of cyclical fluctuations of outside clearings before World War I was characterized by long expansions and short and relatively mild contractions. During the expansion phase, outside clearings rose on the average 32.7 percentage points (in terms of the cyclical average), while during the contraction they declined only 13.4 points.

The cyclical fluctuations of the outside clearings series, however, did not coincide exactly with the turning points of general business. At all 11 troughs identified by the National Bureau of Economic Research, outside clearings began to rise earlier than general business; this lead (ranging from one to ten months) averaged six months. At the peak, the outside clearings series lagged in eight out of ten cases; the average lag was two months. These lead-and-lag relationships

---

[7] Several investigators working independently and using different lists of time series (in some cases including clearings) have almost invariably recognized the same expansions and contractions. See Arthur F. Burns and Wesley C. Mitchell, *Measuring Business Cycles*, Table 27. For a revised list of peaks and troughs, see U.S. Department of Commerce, *Historical Statistics of the United States, 1789-1945*, p. 320.

[8] The author gratefully acknowledges the considerable help received from the National Bureau of Economic Research, which put at his disposal the analyses and the supporting charts of the several clearings and debits series discussed in this chapter. With the exception of Macaulay's series for outside clearings not adjusted for trend, the discussion is based on turning points determined by the staff of the National Bureau. The turning points in Macaulay's unadjusted series were determined by the author, using the Bureau's rules as summarized by Burns and Mitchell in *Measuring Business Cycles*.

[9] While the outside clearings series begins in 1875, it does not reach the first cyclical trough before May 1878. All series referred to in this chapter have been analyzed on a daily average basis.

reflect the strong upward trend in the series (no clear lead or lag relationships were found for the interwar period when the series was not subject to secular growth). As the coverage of the clearings series increased over time, aggregate clearings turned upward during the last stage of business contraction. On the upper turning point, clearings usually continued to increase for the same reason after general business had already turned downward.[10]

That the leads and lags at turning points are caused partly by the strong upward trend can be shown by comparing the timing, before and after adjustment for trend, of Frickey's series for seven cities (described in Chapter II) at peaks and troughs of aggregate business (for 1884-1914). After adjustment for trend, the pronounced lead at the trough was considerably reduced from 7.1 to 3.6 months. At the peak, the relatively smaller lag of 1.0 was reduced to 0.8 months.[11]

Since periods of increasing and decreasing prices alternated between the end of the Civil War and World War I, deflating the original series shifted the timing of turning points in some cases in one direction, in others in the opposite direction. In most cases, the price correction was too small to change the timing of turning points. Thus in Macaulay's series, deflating by Snyder's index of the general price level did not change the timing at ten cyclical troughs and eight peaks. The timing was changed at one cyclical trough and three peaks only. In all cases the shifts were very small. As a consequence, the average lead at the troughs and the average lag at the peaks were the same for the deflated as for the undeflated series.

Outside clearings have been frequently used after adjustment for both upward trend and the price level. Two variants of this form of the outside clearings series are shown in accompanying Chart VII, Macaulay's deflated and trend-adjusted series and Snyder's "clearings index of business." The two series differ mainly in the trend curve used (a third degree parabolic graduation in Macaulay's and a modified logistic curve in Snyder's), while basic data (Macaulay's)

---

[10] Because of this lead-and-lag relationship at turning points, outside clearings were actually higher at three business cycle troughs (1900, 1904, and 1912) than they had been at the preceding peak.

[11] Similarly, lags and leads in Macaulay's *deflated* series (nine cycles, 1884-1914) are reduced by a trend correction; at the trough the lead is reduced from 5.7 to 4.0 months, while at the peak (omitting the 1900-04 cycle where a different high point is recognized as the peak in the corrected series) the lag is reduced from 4.0 to 0.4.

and the deflator used (Snyder's index of the general price level) are identical, except that Snyder raised Macaulay's clearings series to the level of debits by multiplying it by the constant ratio of 1.14 (the ratio of debits in 140 outside centers to total reported outside clearings during the period 1919-22). As can be seen in the chart, the double correction brings the specific turning points of the clearings series little closer to the business cycle reference dates than does the adjustment for trend alone.

Chart VII
SPECIFIC CYCLES OF SEVEN VARIANTS OF THE OUTSIDE CLEARINGS SERIES
1878-1914

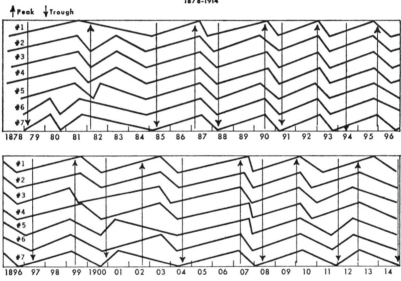

No. 1—*The Commercial and Financial Chronicle.*
No. 2—Macaulay.
No. 3—Frickey.
No. 4—Macaulay, adjusted for price changes.
No. 5—Macaulay, adjusted for price changes and trend.
No. 6—Frickey, adjusted for trend.
No. 7—Snyder's clearings index of business.

Sources.—Files of the National Bureau of Economic Research, except No. 2, turning points of which were determined by the author.

In spite of considerable differences in their respective coverage and in the techniques and time periods used to adjust for seasonal variations and, in some cases, for the trend and for changes in the price level, the turning points of the several series show a clear tendency to bunch within a relatively short span of time. The relatively few differences arise mainly from the fact that technicians of the National Bureau of Economic Research considered certain periods of expansion and contraction in some clearings series as cyclical while other corresponding movements were considered merely as retardations in corresponding phases of longer cycles.[12] Apart from these exceptions, the correspondence in the cyclical contours of the outside clearings series shown in Chart VII is remarkable. All the seven variants in this section show clearly marked cyclical swings closely related to the general fluctuations in aggregate economic activity.

While New York clearings, as discussed more fully elsewhere in this study, were subject not only to changes in the volume of check payments arising from the ebb and flow in general business, but also to the vagaries of trading on the New York Stock Exchange (and other local securities and commodity markets), they nevertheless fluctuated in rather close conformity with the general level of business. During the 60-year period 1855-1914, all turning points in aggregate business are matched by corresponding peaks and troughs in the New York clearing series. Between 1855 and 1914, however, the National Bureau of Economic Research recognizes three cyclical movements in New York clearings (lasting from the trough of October 1873 to April 1876, April 1876 to February 1878, and September 1900 to March 1902, respectively) in addition to 15 cyclical movements corresponding to business cycles. The first two additional movements, following the panic of 1873, reflect possibly speculative activity preceding the resumption of gold specie payments; the third additional cycle occurred during the period of an outburst of speculative activity on the New York Stock Exchange culminating in the panic of May 1901. While in some years the movement of New York clearings was more erratic than that of total outside clearings, the amplitude of random fluctuations, on the whole, was moderate.

---

[12] Thus, for instance, within the span 1878-85 three relatively short wave-like movements occurred. In the *Commercial and Financial Chronicle* series the entire period was considered as a single cyclical entity while in all other variants of the outside clearings series, the National Bureau of Economic Research classified two (but not always the same) of the three movements as cyclical. Another case of marked disagreement occurred in 1899-1900 when the earlier rather than the second low in a double trough was identified as the cyclical trough in Frickey's series unadjusted for trend. Finally, in 1903, in two series the trend adjustment shifted the peak to a secondary high which occurred two years earlier than the cyclical peak in the unadjusted series.

The average rate of growth of New York clearings was faster before 1890 than in the subsequent period, but even in the later period it was almost as rapid as the average rate for outside clearings, although less regular. While, with a single exception, the average level of outside clearings was higher in each successive cycle, in several cycles the average level of New York clearings was lower than in the cycle immediately preceding.

With respect to timing at turning points, New York clearings led at all troughs with the exception of 1855, the average lead having been five months. The lead of New York clearings at the troughs was somewhat smaller than the lead of the outside debits series. Indeed, the average lead of the latter series at troughs during the period 1878-1914 was six months, while New York clearings during the same period led by four months. At the peak, the New York series also had a slight lead (two months) while outside clearings usually lagged at the peak. As in the case of outside clearings, periods of expansion were generally relatively long and those of contraction short, but the discrepancy was somewhat smaller in the New York series.

The period 1919-38. The timing between turning points in the series on deposit money payments and in general business conditions after World War I is shown in Table 9 on page 86. Except at the peak in 1920, the monthly turning points in the outside clearings and debits series coincided exactly in all four full cyclical movements which the two series had in common between the two world wars.[13] The mild cyclical contraction in aggregate economic activity from October 1926 to December 1927, however, was reflected in outside clearings but not in debits, which continued their rapid rate of growth. Outside clearings, on the other hand, began to decline 11 months earlier than aggregate business. They turned upward in January 1927, however, after having declined less than 4 per cent

---

[13] Clearings reached a peak two months after the January 1920 reference date, but debits not until July. Actually, both the unadjusted and the seasonally adjusted outside debits series reached a peak in January 1920 but since the cyclical turning points are determined on the basis of three-month averages, July rather than January is recognized as a peak. Between January and July 1920, the centered three-month moving average moves within the narrow range of 562.7 and 625.2. It should be recalled also that during 1920 reported figures reflected the gradual inclusion of various Federal Reserve Banks and branches in the local clearing arrangements (see pp. 12-14).

TABLE 9

BUSINESS CYCLE TURNING POINTS AND TURNING POINTS
IN OUTSIDE CLEARINGS AND DEBITS, 1919-58[1]

Cyclical turning point		Turning point	
		Outside clearings	Outside debits[2]
Trough, April	1919	November 1914	March 1919
Peak, January	1920	March 1920	July 1920
Trough, July	1921	January 1922	January 1922
Peak, April	1923	April 1923	April 1923
Trough, July	1924	June 1924	June 1924
Peak, October	1926	September 1925	[3]
Trough, November	1927	January 1927	[3]
Peak, July	1929	August 1929	August 1929
Trough, March	1933	March 1933	March 1933
Peak, May	1937	March 1937	March 1937
Trough, June	1938	May 1938	May 1938
Peak, November	1948	Analysis discontinued	August 1948
Trough, October	1949		August 1949
Peak, July	1953		[3]
Trough, August	1954		[3]
Peak, July	1957		July 1957
Trough, April	1958		March 1958

[1] As determined by the National Bureau of Economic Research. For clearings, the *Chronicle* series was used.

[2] Debits to total deposit accounts, except interbank, in 140 centers prior to 1938. Debits to demand deposit accounts, except interbank and Government, in 337 centers since 1948. Both series adjusted for seasonal variation.

[3] No corresponding turning point.

from the peak reached in September 1925, and continued to increase through August 1929.[14]

New York debits also failed to show a contraction in 1926-27, but even during the earlier twenties the correspondence with cyclical dates was poor (leads varied from one to eleven months). The 1929 peak did not occur until the stock exchange crash in October (June being the business cycle peak), while during the 1937-38 cycle there

[14] The fact that outside clearings expanded much more slowly than debits during the period of active speculation exemplifies well the influence of technical factors such as bank mergers. See p. 53.

was a three-month lead at both the turning points. The correspondence of cyclical movements in New York clearings after World War I with both debits and aggregate economic activity was equally poor.

Since World War II. With the growth of national output in physical terms, and even more in dollar value, all three series for debits to demand deposits have been rising since the end of World War II. Furthermore, cyclical swings in business conditions have been relatively moderate. As a result, periods of declining business activity appear in the debits series as relatively slight dips superimposed on a general upward movement. Nevertheless, from the business peak reached in November 1948 to the peak in August 1957, each turning point in general business activity is reflected in the seasonally adjusted series for 337 outside centers by a corresponding peak or trough in the same or in the following or preceding month.

SUMMARY

In the period before World War I, cyclical movements in each of the three basic variants of the outside clearings series corresponded to cyclical movements in aggregate economic activity. Although the turning points in outside clearings usually occurred several months earlier or later than the monthly cyclical dates, lags at peaks and leads at troughs were rather systematic. A good deal of justification for the reliance of students of business fluctuations on outside clearings prior to World War I, therefore, can be found in the retrospective comparison of the cyclical conformity of this series with the contours of economic change over a span of time for which few comprehensive (particularly monthly) economic statistics are available.

For the period between the world wars, Table 9 shows clearly that any reliance placed on outside debits as a single-variable indicator of business conditions would not yield a satisfactory monthly chronology of cyclical movements of aggregate business. In the years following World War II, debits data correspond more closely with the timing of turning points in general business conditions. Some of the difficulties involved in balancing the advantages and short-comings of debits for cyclical analysis, however, will be discussed in Chapter VIII.

DEBITS AND CLEARINGS

The superiority of debits over clearings on grounds of greater uniformity of items covered, and of greater independence from changes in banking structure and in techniques of collecting out-of-town checks, seems to have little practical bearing on the sensitivity of either series to cyclical change. In most cyclical movements since the end of World War I, clearings and debits (adjusted for seasonal variations) began to rise and to fall in the same month. Furthermore, while outside clearings fluctuated somewhat more widely than corresponding debits, the difference between percentage changes of the two series was, on the whole, slight. Indeed, as has been shown in Chapter IV, the ratio of outside clearings to debits was subject to only gradual shifts.

VII. The Velocity of Deposits

The rate of turnover of bank deposits is an important tool for analyzing the behavior of money. The various measures of this rate are not reported directly by banking institutions, as is the case with the debits and clearing series discussed in earlier chapters, but are derived by relating debits or clearings to the volume of bank deposits.

TIME SERIES ON DEPOSIT VELOCITY

The first attempt to estimate the velocity of demand deposits in the United States was made by Irving Fisher in 1911.[1] Earlier, Edwin W. Kemmerer had attempted to estimate the velocity of currency circulation for the single year 1896 by dividing the estimated volume of total money payments (MV) by the amount of money in circulation, but had made no such attempt for check payments. Referring to Pierre des Essars' computations of the rapidity of turnover of bank deposits in France, Kemmerer remarked that "unfortunately data for such an investigation are unavailable for the banks of England and the United States."[2]

Irving Fisher. The missing link in Kemmerer's estimates—the volume of bank deposits subject to check—was provided by Irving Fisher.[3] He derived a series of "individual deposits subject to check" from figures on "individual deposits" given in annual reports of the Comptroller of the Currency by making several adjustments involving rough estimates. The statistical data on which Fisher based his

---

[1] For a general survey and bibliography, see H. Neisser, "Umlaufsgeschwindigkeit der Bankdepositen," *Handwörterbuch des Bankwesens*, pp. 567-72. For an exhaustive critical review of the literature on this subject, see Arthur W. Marget, *The Theory of Prices*, Vol. I, especially Chap. XI.

[2] *Money and Credit Instruments in Their Relation to General Prices*, p. 116, footnote. Subsequent quotations are from the second edition (1909) in which some statistical material was carried forward a few years. The first statistical investigation of the velocity of deposits (deposits of the Bank of France, from 1810 to 1892, and of other continental central banks) was made by Pierre des Essars. See "La Vitesse de la circulation de la monnaie," *Journal de la Société de Statistique de Paris*, April 1895, p. 149.

[3] *The Purchasing Power of Money*. The measurement of velocity of check money by the ratio of clearings to average deposits was apparently first suggested by Dr. John M. Gaines of Yale University, whose unpublished lectures are mentioned by John Pease Norton in *Statistical Studies in the New York Money Market Preceded by a Brief Analysis under the Theory of Money and Credit*. In the first part of this study, Norton developed Newcomb's equation of "societary circulation" into a formidable formula into which several categories of currency and of deposits and their velocities enter as independent variables. While specifically referring to various relevant statistical data, and actually quoting some figures, Norton did not actually estimate the magnitude of the various elements entering into the equation. His remarkable study was apparently written under the influence of Professor Fisher, one of his teachers at Yale, whose early writings on the equation of exchange he quotes.

estimates of the volume of check payments covering the years 1896-1909 were no less precarious than those used by Kemmerer, although Fisher had two available benchmarks instead of one. As a starting point, he estimated for two different years the dollar volume of checks deposited in a single day (on the settling day nearest July 1, 1896—the date used by Kemmerer—and on March 16, 1909, based on Kinley's estimates made for the National Monetary Commission). As the next step, he estimated the annual volume of check circulation. Fisher then used a weighted average of New York and outside clearings to interpolate the estimated volume of check payments in the intervening years (1897-1908). The ratio of check payments to deposits yielded an estimate of the annual rate of turnover of "deposits subject to check" ranging between 36 and 54, and showing a clear cyclical pattern. Fisher thought that the probable error ranged between about 5 and 10 per cent.

Federal Reserve Bank of New York. Later studies by the staff of the Federal Reserve Bank of New York found that in the first five years following World War I the velocity of bank deposits in the United States (monthly data) fluctuated within the range estimated by Fisher for an earlier period. In the early twenties, the Bank's research staff initiated work on the rate of deposit turnover "not simply as a means of filling in one of the gaps in our knowledge of the factors in the equation of exchange, but more largely because of the significance of velocity in any consideration of changes in the credit situation."[4] Monthly velocity figures were computed for New York City and seven other centers (Albany, Buffalo, Rochester, Syracuse, Boston, Chicago, and San Francisco) according to a formula worked out jointly by Irving Fisher, Edwin W. Kemmerer, and J. H. Riddle. The rate of turnover of demand deposits (beginning with 1919) was computed for each city by relating "debits to individual accounts" to net demand deposits at a group of identical banks. In computing both the numerator and the denominator of the ratio, certain assumptions had to be made and estimates had to be used instead of reported figures.[5]

---

[4] W. Randolph Burgess, "Velocity of Bank Deposits," *Journal of the American Statistical Association,* June 1923, p. 728. See also "Velocity of Bank Deposits," *Federal Reserve Bulletin,* May 1923, pp. 562-66.

[5] Data on net demand deposits (which prior to the Banking Act of 1935 did not include U.S. Government deposits) were obtained from reports filed with the individual Reserve Banks. Because of the different member bank practices of reporting deposits, it was impossible to estimate exactly demand deposits ex-

In the following year, however, the index for the eight cities was abandoned in favor of an index with a broader basis. Demand deposits were reported at that time by about 800 banks in 101 leading centers and debits by an even larger number of institutions in 141 centers. Restricting the velocity index to institutions that reported both demand deposits and debits would have involved a considerable volume of clerical work. Since the analytical interest was focused on fluctuations in the velocity of bank deposits rather than on the exact annual rate of deposit turnover, a systematic bias was accepted for the sake of simplifying and speeding up computations. The new variant of the index of velocity of bank deposits, therefore, combined monthly estimates derived from weekly data for two groups of institutions that were not completely identical, although the bulk of deposits was held by banks which also reported debits. For the sake of simplicity in computation, the adjustments formerly made in the eight-city index (elimination of interbank deposits and of debits to United States Government and time deposit accounts) were not continued.

For the period prior to 1919, the new index was extended by Snyder by using clearings (instead of debits) and total deposits in all national banks (including time, Government, and interbank deposits as well as individual demand deposits).[6] This extended index, which was compiled for 1875-1918, was based to an even larger degree than the index for the period following World War I on two series covering groups of banks that were far from identical and that were affected by growth factors of different intensity. The gradual extension of the coverage of the clearings series resulting from the addition of new centers and accessions to clearing house membership in cities already reporting was moderate on the whole, since about half of all United States clearings was represented by

clusive of interbank deposits. Debits to individual demand deposit accounts were estimated by subtracting from reported total debits (1) withdrawals from Federal Government accounts (for which exact figures were available at the Federal Reserve Banks) and (2) estimated debits to time deposits (which on the basis of data obtained from six New York City banks for a number of different periods were estimated to turn over on an average of twice a year).

The errors introduced by making several assumptions and estimates were considered to be too small to have material effect on the velocity figures obtained. It was conceded, though, that the underestimation of net demand deposits in financial centers tended to increase the velocity figures obtained for such cities in relation to those for smaller cities. The individual velocity indexes for the eight cities were adjusted for seasonal variation and were subsequently combined into a national index by assigning the weight of .45 to the New York series and the weight of .55 to the seven other cities. See Snyder, "Deposit Activity as a Measure of Business Activity," *Review of Economic Statistics*, October 1924, pp. 253-57.

[6] *Ibid.*, p. 255.

New York exchanges and an additional large proportion of estimated total United States clearings was accounted for by other large financial centers already reporting in 1875. Aggregate deposits of national banks, however, had been increasing more rapidly than those of all banks. Consequently, the index based on the ratio of total clearings to deposits at national banks showed a slow, irregular, secular decline. Instead of the original ratios, Snyder therefore presented deviations from a seven-year moving average.

Although nowhere explicitly stated, Snyder's clearings index prior to 1919 evidently reflected the combined velocity of individual and interbank deposits (since interbank balances and checks drawn against them are included in the basic data).

Snyder's original index of the rate of deposit turnover thus consists of two segments: for 1875-1918, it represents deviations from a seven-year moving average, while for the years since 1919 it is an index with the 1919-23 average as a base. For both segments seasonal variations have been eliminated and a three-month moving average placed at the last month has been taken "to eliminate occasional erratic and quite inexplicable movements of clearings." After comparing for 1919-23 the velocity index with his own index of the volume of trade, Snyder concluded "that the activity of bank deposits is actually a feasible measure of business activity and, with due reservations as to the limitations of the method, may usefully be so employed."[7]

In 1936 a major revision of the velocity indexes was undertaken by the Federal Reserve Bank of New York (limited to data beginning in 1919) in order to achieve greater consistency between numerator and denominator. Centers for which demand deposits were not available were eliminated. While this was a definite improvement, complete comparability was not achieved since some member banks in the 100 centers outside New York City (mostly the smaller institutions) were reporting deposits but not weekly debits;[8] on the other hand, some banks that were not members of the Federal Reserve

---

[7] Described in detail in the *Journal of the American Statistical Association*, December 1923, pp. 949-63.

[8] For New York City turnover rates were computed directly from debit and deposit reports received from member banks. Deposits of 16 and debits at 20 banks were used. Data from institutions that subsequently began to report debits were disregarded.

System were reporting debits, but not deposits.[9] Notwithstanding the several successive improvements which made the divisor and the dividend more nearly comparable, the resulting ratio was still not an exact measure of the rate of deposit turnover.

When the series for weekly reporting member banks in leading cities was revised in 1947, the Federal Reserve Bank of New York decided to use the Board's series on the velocity of demand deposits (described below) as a basis for its indexes. Consequently, since July 1946 the indexes published by the Federal Reserve Bank of New York represent merely the velocity series of the Board of Governors adjusted for seasonal variation. These indexes were recomputed back to 1935 and linked to the old index (available since 1919).

Angell. In 1936 also, James W. Angell published for the period 1921-34 weekly indexes of the velocity of "circulating deposits," defined as net demand deposits plus United States Government deposits and items in process of collection minus net balances due to banks.[10] Angell's method was similar to that of the Federal Reserve Bank of New York. But while the latter tried to achieve the greatest degree of comparability of divisor and dividend by eliminating from the debits series for 140 outside centers all cities in which no banks reporting weekly demand deposit figures were located, Angell, following Snyder's earlier work, computed ratios of debits in 140 reporting outside centers to deposits in weekly reporting member banks in 100 cities, without any adjustments. Since the two series did not relate to an identical group of banks, the series of ratios obtained was an index of velocity rather than a true measure of velocity itself. Angell also constructed a similar index for New York City. Because in New York City the bulk of reported debits and deposits related to identical banks, he considered this index to

---

[9] Beginning in 1934 demand deposits adjusted had been substituted for net demand deposits. Net demand deposits exclude interbank deposits and items in process of collection. Demand deposits adjusted exclude interbank deposits, deposits of the U.S. Government, and items in process of collection. Demand deposits adjusted include certified checks, cashiers' and officers' checks, outstanding letters of credit, and travelers' checks (including those sold for cash), which when paid do not give rise to debits to individual accounts. For a discussion of the two definitions, see *Federal Reserve Bulletin*, October 1941, pp. 990-91. A minor refinement in the velocity series of the Federal Reserve Bank of New York was introduced in 1942 by eliminating from debits estimated withdrawals from war loan accounts.

[10] *The Behavior of Money*, pp. 93-128 and notes to Appendix B, Table VI, pp. 186-88. When Angell's study was in progress, the current series of "demand deposits adjusted" was not computed regularly. Even the series on net demand deposits, as compiled at that time, required considerable adjustment before it could be used as a denominator in the velocity ratio. Also, since the weekly debits series for 141 cities was not available prior to 1923, Angell omitted data for the years 1919-20 as "not available" and estimated for 1921-23 debits in 141 cities from the total for *all* reporting centers.

reflect "very nearly the true exchange velocity figures." Before Angell's study came off the press, a new series of adjusted demand deposits began to be released regularly by the Board of Governors of the Federal Reserve System, and the Federal Reserve Bank of New York was able to substitute demand deposits adjusted for net demand deposits, as indicated in footnote 9 on page 93.

Board of Governors of the Federal Reserve System. Another monthly series on the turnover of bank deposits was inaugurated (and made available back to 1935) by the Board of Governors in 1944, after it began to collect debits to demand deposit accounts, except interbank and United States Government accounts, at weekly reporting member banks in 101 centers. This series was obtained from the same banks that report data on demand deposits and the two series are, therefore, strictly comparable. Annual ratios of turnover of demand deposits (separately for New York and the outside centers) were computed by taking into account the number of business days, but they are not adjusted for seasonal variation. In contrast to the old series of the Federal Reserve Bank of New York, *gross* deposits rather than net deposits adjusted were used as the divisor.

Finally, the Board of Governors also estimates the rates of turnover of total and of demand deposits for *all* commercial banks. Such estimates involve the "blowing up" of the available series on deposits and debits.[11] They are available from 1919, on an annual basis only.

After consolidation of the weekly and monthly debits series, the new series has served as a basis for the computation of annual rates of deposit turnover for the three breakdowns now published.[12] Since demand deposits (for the end of month) are obtained from all banks reporting debits, the problem of differences in the coverage of the numerator and the denominator, which caused so much trouble when the Federal Reserve Bank of New York began computing velocity indexes, does not exist any more. There remain, however, other computational difficulties which should be kept in mind when

---

[11] As described in detail in *Banking and Monetary Statistics*, pp. 232-33.

[12] For 1943 to 1952, a monthly turnover series (for New York and all other centers) of total deposits was published by the Board of Governors in connection with the then current monthly, except interbank, debits to total deposits series.

interpreting changes in rates of deposit turnover as well as their absolute level.

First, since it is impossible to allocate items in process of collection to United States Government, all other demand and inter-bank deposits, *gross* rather than net deposits adjusted are used as a divisor. Hence the divisor of the fraction is too large, and the published series somewhat underestimates the actual rate of turnover. Since the difference between gross and net demand deposits is very small, it is unlikely that a significant seasonal or cyclical bias is introduced in this manner. Second, the average of deposits at the beginning and at the end of the month is used to measure the average level of deposits. Daily averages may differ from such estimated levels, in particular in months when large tax payments are due. Third, a uniform number of working days (allowing for Sundays and the eight so-called universal holidays) is used. The level of debits is, however, also influenced by other holidays observed locally and by Saturday closings (and in some instances—closings on other days) which have spread since World War II and have now become almost

TABLE 10

SUMMARY OF MONTHLY VELOCITY SERIES

Description	Period for which available	Dividend	Divisor	Remarks
Indexes of deposit velocity: New York City 93 outside centers[1]	1919– Feb. 1953	Debits to demand deposit accounts, except interbank and U.S. Government[2]	Demand deposits adjusted[3]	Adjusted for seasonal variation
Annual rate of turnover of total deposits, except interbank: New York City 341 other centers[5]	1943– Feb. 1953	Debits to total deposits accounts, except interbank	Total deposits, except interbank[4]	Debits adjusted for number of business days in month
Annual rate of turnover of demand deposits, except interbank and U.S. Government:[6] New York City 6 other financial centers 337 other centers	1935 to date	Debits to demand deposit accounts, except interbank and U.S. Government	Gross demand deposits	Adjusted for number of business days in month

[1] Prior to June 1947, 100 centers. Published by the Federal Reserve Bank of New York.
[2] Prior to 1935, debits to total deposit accounts, except interbank.
[3] Prior to 1935, estimated net demand deposits.
[4] Partly estimated.
[5] 332 centers December 1947 through December 1950, and 333 centers prior to December 1947.
[6] Prior to 1953, monthly debits estimated from prorated weekly data for New York City and 93 (prior to June 1947—100) outside centers. Also available adjusted for seasonal variation.

universal in several important States. In part because of the uncertain impact of Saturday closings, the problem of a seasonal adjustment for the velocity series has not yet been solved satisfactorily.[13]

THE BEHAVIOR OF THE VELOCITY OF DEPOSITS

Changes in the velocity of bank deposits may result from changes in the amount of deposits or in the volume of check payments, or from a combination of both factors. Deposits and debits have sometimes moved in the same direction and sometimes in opposite directions (as during the recessions of 1953-54 and 1957-58). There have been periods (such as the years 1925-29) when the amount of demand deposits has fluctuated (mainly for seasonal reasons) within a very narrow range, while debits have increased rapidly.

Despite the considerable interest of monetary economists in the exchange velocity of deposits, established knowledge in this field has considerable gaps. Angell thoroughly studied the seasonal behavior of the indexes of deposit velocity and he and a number of other students studied their cyclical fluctuations.[14] Considerable uncertainty exists, however, with respect to the long-term trend of the velocity of demand deposits.

Long-term movements. As pointed out by A. G. Hart, Irving Fisher's analysis of the elements determining the velocity of deposit turnover implies a rising trend.[15] The reason is that, with one possible exception, all pertinent factors acting upon velocity listed by Fisher may be expected to change in a direction which would cause velocity of circulation to increase.[16] Snyder rightly explained the irregular secular decline shown by his index from the 1870's through World War I by imperfections in the underlying statistical series.[17] Since his main interest was the cyclical behavior of the index, he was satisfied with using a moving average to obtain cyclical deviations and concluded that "there is no discoverable secular trend or change.[18] Chandler claims that "for several reasons, V (velocity of total money supply) also tends to show an upward long-term trend

---

[13] Currently, work is in progress to develop seasonal factors based on the regression technique suggested by H. Eisenpress (see p. 80, footnote 6).

[14] *The Behavior of Money*, especially Chap. IV.

[15] *Money, Debt and Economic Activity*, 1953 edition, pp. 161-63.

[16] *The Purchasing Power of Money*, p. 79.

[17] *Review of Economic Statistics*, October 1924, p. 255.

[18] "New Measures of the Equation of Exchange," *American Economic Review*, December 1924, p. 699.

in a growing economy," but gives no statistical evidence for his belief.[19] Burns, however, expressed the opinion that for the twenties "there is no evidence of a secular advance in V" (velocity of deposits).[20]

Actually, since a reliable series of total deposits subject to check is not available for years prior to 1919, satisfactory basic data for indexes of deposit turnover can be obtained for the period after World War I only. During this period the rate of turnover was lower in the thirties and the forties than in the twenties but, since this difference can be explained by factors which were not at work prior to World War I, it provides no clue to the pattern of velocity changes prior to 1914.

The cyclical behavior of Snyder's index of deposit velocity has been analyzed by the National Bureau of Economic Research for the years 1875 through 1943.[21] In the period between the resumption of gold specie payments and the outbreak of World War II, with two exceptions (the mild 1924-27 cycle and the 1933-38 cycle), clearly defined wavelike movements in the rate of deposit turnover corresponded to each business cycle.

In each case, deposit activity typically began to rise and also to turn downward in advance of general business activity. The pattern showed a continuous increase of velocity (the cyclical average being equal to 100) to a peak of 116.7; the subsequent decline was also gradual and somewhat slower. This pattern was rather consistent, a sharp increase in the last phase of expansion occurring in 12 out of 16 cyclical movements recognized in Snyder's velocity series. Similarly, the sharp drop in the first phase was observed in 9 out of 16 periods of contraction. When movements of the index of deposit activity were studied within the cyclical periods of aggregate business (as delineated by the National Bureau of Economic Research turning points), the amplitude of the cyclical movements of the index of deposit activity was reduced and the sharp rise preceding the peak disappeared.

---

[19] Lester V. Chandler, *The Economics of Money and Banking*, p. 565.

[20] Arthur F. Burns, "The Quantity Theory and Price Stabilization," *American Economic Review*, December 1929, p. 572. See also his note, "The Relative Importance of Check and Cash Payments," *Journal of the American Statistical Association*, December 1929, p. 424.

[21] For the period 1875-1918, this index represents deviations from a seven-year moving average.

The increased use made of bank deposits immediately after the reopening of banks following the bank holiday of 1933 and the sharp drop in deposits (as many banks remained closed) resulted in a sharp peak in the index in July, followed by a more or less gradual decline until the beginning of the defense period; the 1937 peak in general business was not reflected in the velocity of either outside or New York deposits.

During the years of World War II, during which the money supply more than doubled, deposit turnover rates continued to decline for outside demand deposits, but rose slightly in New York, as Chart VIII shows. Both series showed sharp peaks during the periods of successive war bond drives, but otherwise remained close to the lowest levels reached at the end of the thirties.

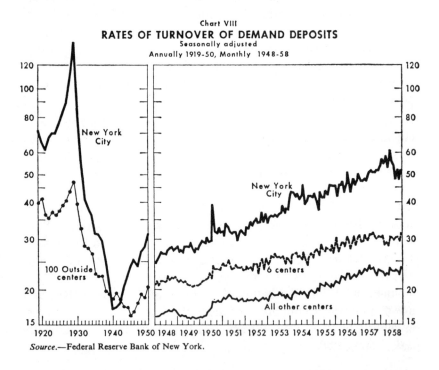

Chart VIII
RATES OF TURNOVER OF DEMAND DEPOSITS
Seasonally adjusted
Annually 1919-50, Monthly 1948-58

Source.—Federal Reserve Bank of New York.

The excess liquidity which resulted from war financing prevented any appreciable rise in velocity until the end of the 1949 recession, which was clearly reflected in the New York series as well as in the two series for outside centers. After the outbreak of the Korean conflict, velocity of outside demand deposits (6 financial as well as the 337 remaining centers) rose and in subsequent years continued to increase fairly steadily, the 1953-54 and 1957-58 recessions being marked by almost imperceptible dips. The rate of rise accelerated during the most recent period of money restraint when the rates of turnover rose about one-fourth from the end of 1954 to the middle of 1957; they declined during the subsequent period of ease through the middle of 1958. New York rates of deposit turnover rose more rapidly and after 1955 reacted even more vigorously to the restraint placed on the growth of the money supply. They rose through the end of 1957 to a level twice as high as during the war and first post-war years,[22] while deposits in the 6 outside centers as well as in the 337 other centers were used only about half again as actively as at the end of the war.

Variations in rate of turnover. Considerable knowledge of the relationship of deposit velocity to size and location of bank, and of the differences between the velocity of time deposits, demand deposits (other than interbank deposits), and interbank deposits was gained from unpublished studies by Victor Longstreet and Robert Fenn (then of the staff of the Board of Governors). These studies were based largely on material collected specifically for this purpose from a large group of leading member banks. The main result established by the Longstreet-Fenn inquiry was the existence of rather wide differences in the rate of turnover of demand deposits during the decade studied (1925-34), particularly in predepression years when deposits were more active.[23] It appeared clear that deposits were generally more active in the larger cities than in the smaller, and in the larger banks than in the smaller institutions. Since large banks are usually located in large cities, both relationships most likely reflect the same underlying factors. In addition to city size, the average annual rate of (gross) deposit turnover in individual cities was

---

[22] See "Money Supply and Velocity," *Monthly Review of the Federal Reserve Bank of Kansas City,* December 1956. For a discussion of the New York series, see "The Velocity of Demand Deposits in New York City," *Monthly Review of the Federal Reserve Bank of New York,* May 1953.

[23] *The Cleveland Trust Company Business Bulletin,* Apr. 15, 1929, compares a computed rate of turnover of bank deposits for the six Federal Reserve districts in which about 90 per cent of all stock tickers are located with the rate for the other six districts. It is shown that from 1924 to the beginning of 1929 the rate of turnover nearly doubled in the first group of districts but remained steady in the second group until a very slight increase began in 1928.

related to the reserve classification of banks and to the character of the city in which the banks were located or of the surrounding agricultural region.

These conclusions were confirmed by studies conducted more recently by the Federal Reserve System. A wide spread in turnover rates of demand deposits, except interbank and Government, was found among member banks reporting debits on the basis of data covering July 1955 to June 1956. In 12 per cent of the banks, demand deposits turned over less than once a month, but in a small group of institutions (less than 5 per cent of those reporting) turnover rates two and a half times as large or more were found. There is a clear correlation between rate of turnover and total deposit size of reporting institutions (which presumably would hold or become even more pronounced if banks were classified by size of demand deposits only). The same correlation was found within each of the three reserve classifications. Almost all central reserve city banks, especially the very large ones, showed very high turnover rates. However, a substantial proportion of institutions in the country bank category have also fairly high turnover rates.

A parallel analysis of all reporting banks, classified by the size of demand deposits alone, shows a systematic relationship between rates of deposit turnover and size of reporting unit.[24] There is no clear indication that turnover rates are related to the population size of center in which the bank is located, although on the surface such relationship seems to exist. In effect, it merely reflects the fact that the larger banking institutions are usually located in large cities and thus influence turnover rates computed for these centers.

Differences in rates of deposit turnover reflect variations in the composition of deposits by holder type, since typical rates of turnover associated with business accounts are not the same as those shown by personal or State and municipal deposits, or those of nonprofit institutions. There are evidently wide variations in the rate of deposit use within each broad holder category, depending on industry affiliation, size of account, cash management policies, etc. The

---

[24] Demand deposits of individuals, partnerships and corporations, and of States and political subdivisions, the two subtotals for which debits are currently reported. This analysis was based on reporting units which, in the case of banks with branches, are not identical with the reporting bank; only those branches of a bank which are located in the reporting center were included in the reporting unit.

association of velocity rates with certain characteristics of banks, such as size or location, exists, indeed, merely because depositors of certain kinds of banks tend to have common characteristics. Thus, for instance, banks in small communities have typically a large proportion of farm depositors. The contribution of financial debits to New York City totals and the exceedingly high rate of turnover of demand deposit accounts of selected categories of New York financial firms have already been discussed in Chapter III.

VIII.   Analysis of Business Fluctuations

What use has been made of clearings and debits? For what purposes have they been used in the various fields of economic analysis? By whom and with what success? These and a host of other questions may be raised with almost any economic time series that has been widely used—or misused. Since no other group of time series has been used as generally and as intensively in studies of business fluctuations as statistics of the use of deposit money, the present chapter will be confined to the discussion of some outstanding examples of the use made of clearings and debits.

The use of clearings and debits statistics for analytical purposes has undergone a significant change which is easily traceable to the increase in the wealth of comprehensive statistical data available for business and monetary analysis. The high point in the use of debits as a national indicator of business came in the twenties and thirties. Subsequently, with the development of national income statistics and the related system of social accounts, much less reliance has been placed on the national debits series. An important new use of debits developed after the end of World War II, when substantial interest in regional and local analysis developed. More recently, the focus has been on turnover ratios derived from debits, rather than on debits directly. The use of velocity data is discussed in the following chapter.

CLEARINGS AND DEBITS IN STUDIES OF BUSINESS CYCLES

Students of business cycles have regarded clearings and debits as one of the most comprehensive general indicators of the "state of trade," particularly in long-range studies. The use made of clearings and debits statistics by three outstanding students of business cycles— Wesley C. Mitchell, Joseph A. Schumpeter, and Edwin R. Frickey— reviewed below, is representative of a much broader body of empirical investigations using these series.

Mitchell. In his search for time series that would reflect cyclical fluctuations in the physical and monetary volume of business, Mitchell, in his pioneering *Business Cycles*, selected two series, bank clearings and gross earnings of railroads, as representative of the state of domestic trade. "Since every business enterprise of any size directly or indirectly makes use of the railways on the one hand and on the other hand of the banks, the records of railway traffic and bank transactions afford perhaps the best single gauges of the amount of business going on within the limits of a country."[1] After comparing New York clearings with the *number* (rather than *value*) of shares sold on the New York Stock Exchange, and drawing attention to the speculative transactions in clearings, Mitchell concluded that "the contribution made by the Stock Exchange to bank clearings is so huge as to invalidate the use of the New York figures as a gauge of the activity of general business."

In discussing cyclical fluctuations in the monetary field, Mitchell found that the annual ratios of check clearings to estimated average bank deposits in New York, Boston, and Philadelphia for 1890-1911, which he computed, amply confirmed "Fisher's conclusion that the velocity of check circulation rises in prosperity and sinks in depression." Mitchell's *Business Cycles* thus illustrates the two main uses later made of clearings and debits in business cycle research— as indicators of general business conditions and as measures of changes in the exchange velocity of money.

When 14 years later Mitchell published his second major contribution on economic fluctuations, he again drew heavily on clearings and debits statistics.[2] As a matter of fact, all seven United States indexes of business conditions discussed in the chapter "The Contribution of Statistics" are either indexes of clearings and debits (Snyder's "clearings index of business" and Frickey's "index of outside clearings") or composite indexes into which clearings (or debits) enter as one of the main components (Persons' index of trade, his index of general business conditions, Snyder's index of deposit activity, his index of the volume of trade, and, prior to 1918, the A. T. and T. index of general business). Mitchell's numerous calculations on changes in direction, timing, and duration of business cycles in the United States are based on five of those seven series,

---

[1] Wesley C. Mitchell, *Business Cycles*, p. 242. Mitchell reproduced the aggregate annual clearings outside New York (contrasting them with New York and London clearings), as compiled by the *Commercial and Financial Chronicle*.
[2] *Business Cycles, The Problem and Its Setting.*

including three clearings series. In another important chapter of the volume, dealing with economic organization and business cycles, Mitchell used Burgess' and Snyder's studies (including some hitherto unpublished material supplied by Snyder) of the velocity of circulation.

Clearings and debits series were intensively studied by the National Bureau of Economic Research, as may be seen from the numerous charts and tables in Burns' and Mitchell's *Measuring Business Cycles*. Clearings and debits series provided the raw materials for the testing of the several hypotheses on the effects of various statistical techniques (choice of time unit, trend adjustments, smoothing and use of averages) on the results of cyclical analysis. Snyder's deflated clearings were also used in the last three chapters to determine whether substantial secular change can be detected in cyclical behavior, to test the hypothesis that business cycles are minor subdivisions of "major" cycles, and to test the stability of cyclical patterns in successive cycles. Considerable use was made of clearings and debits in Mitchell's posthumous *What Happens during Business Cycles*.

Schumpeter. The time series on deposit-money transactions were also generously used in another important contribution to the study of economic fluctuations, Schumpeter's *Business Cycles*. Schumpeter did not use statistical data in the same systematic fashion as Mitchell, but rather resorted to statistical series for testing one or another hypothesis, or merely for illustrating a point.

Relatively few economic series go far enough into the past to afford an opportunity to discuss "Kondratieffs," the longest of the three types of periodic nonseasonal fluctuations which Schumpeter's model involves; clearings, however, are one of them. Moreover, their use in his study is amply justified by the importance which, according to Schumpeter, clearings and debits assume in the minds of entrepreneurs, the motor of economic development in Schumpeterian economics. In the introduction, Schumpeter drew up a list from "businessmen's discussions, the business pages of the daily press, circulars of banks and other concerns, trade journals, and so on . . . of what most people agree are relevant facts illustrative of business situations." High on this list, Schumpeter placed New York and outside bank clearings and debits, noting that these series are "often mentioned in reply to the request to give precision to such terms as 'business activity' or 'volume of business'."[3]

Schumpeter drew upon clearings and debits in the chapters dealing with the period prior to World War I as well as in those dealing with the interwar period. In each case, after examining the cyclical behavior of price series and of physical quantities, Schumpeter proceeded to analyze what he called "system expenditure" (consumers' plus producers' expenditures). Schumpeter held debits to banking accounts to be "the most comprehensive series of expenditure."[4] For the period before World War I he used the clearings series which "has been shown to display so close a relation to . . . debits since the war."

A large part of the chapter on "Expenditure, Wages, Customers' Balances" was built around an analysis of Frickey's series of outside clearings. Schumpeter discussed more carefully than many other students who made analytical use of outside clearings the limitations of those data, and he also indicated in which respects they differ from aggregate expenditures. Recognizing the limitations of the clearings series arising from institutional factors, including changes in habits of payments, Schumpeter concluded that fluctuations in the clearings series were "quite satisfactorily accounted for" by his model and that it "does not obviously indicate any other than a passive role of money and credit."[5] The supporting data were presented in a chart covering the years 1890-1913 where, in order to show their representativeness for the dollar volume of physical production, outside clearings were compared graphically with (1) Persons' index of manufacturing and mining multiplied by the Bureau of Labor Statistics index of wholesale prices, (2) Douglas' payroll series, and (3) a series of "net" deposits minus investments at all national banks outside New York City. In another chart Schumpeter compared the clearings series for a longer period, 1875-1913, with (1) pig-iron consumption, (2) Hoover's index of pro-

---

[3] Joseph A. Schumpeter, *Business Cycles*, Vol. 1, pp. 15-17. The parenthetical remark that clearings and debits are "attended to only by Americans, excepting the case of a Hamburg merchant who was, however, thoroughly familiar with the usual methods of business cycle analysis," seems to belong to the category of provocative exaggerations. The contrasting of city with "provincial" clearings, for instance, is familiar from British business cycle literature.

[4] *Ibid.*, p. 550.

[5] *Ibid.*, p. 554.

duction of capital equipment, (3) deposits outside New York City, and (4) loans and discounts outside New York City (the two latter series from A. A. Young's analysis of national bank data). Two more charts for the period prior to World War I were also organized around the clearing series.

In the chapter devoted to a close examination of the period following World War I (1919-29) Schumpeter relied, in the section devoted to system expenditure, on outside debits to the same extent that he drew upon clearings for the earlier period. Monthly outside debits, which he rightly held to be more dependable than the clearings used for the earlier period, were compared for the years 1919-35 with (1) outside net demand deposits, (2) national income (adjusted to exclude imputed items), (3) an index of payrolls in manufacturing, and (4) hourly earnings in manufacturing.[6]

In analyzing the clearings series, Schumpeter found that "not only the properties to be expected from our model do actually show, but also that it behaves much as if no other influences than those embodied in our model had acted upon it." The shorter cycles (the 40-month Kitchins and the Juglars containing three Kitchins) in the clearings series could be dated by Schumpeter rather easily, but the Kondratieffs (of about 60 years' duration) presented more of a problem since a definite break in the gradient of the trend occurred during the nineties (between the second and the third long wave). Schumpeter was so impressed by the way in which fluctuations in clearings conformed to his model that he concluded that the "problem is not so much how to explain deviations from that [his theoretical] expectation as how to explain a conformity so much beyond reasonable hope."[7] Schumpeter's whole discussion stresses the general conformity of the outside clearings series with other significant series, as well as its responsiveness to cyclical fluctuations rather than any definite lead relationship.[8]

Frickey. Unlike Schumpeter's *Business Cycles*, Frickey's study

---

[6] An interesting use is made of outside clearings in order to substantiate Schumpeter's contention that the traditional distinction between demand and time deposits is too rigid and that "in the twenties time and demand deposits were essentially the same kind of thing" (p. 856). By treating time deposits on the same footing with demand deposits, the question of why velocity increased during the twenties was disposed of.

[7] *Ibid.*, p. 581.

[8] A digression in this chapter involved the application of Georgescu's period analysis to Philadelphia clearings (Chart XXIV) "for the sake of displaying an ingenious method rather than for the results that can be gathered from it."

of economic fluctuations in the United States during the 50-year period prior to World War I is a major statistical undertaking. The main part of this study involves derivation of a "standard pattern" of cyclical fluctuations. For deriving such a pattern, Frickey selected, "on the basis of fundamental importance, continuity and homogeneity," 13 time series, among which he included New York and outside clearings.[9] In addition to the 13 series, Frickey examined a large body of supplementary data, among which Snyder's index of deflated clearings was selected as "the only index which can be regarded as in any sense comprehensive with reference to the volume of trade."[10]

ECONOMIC ANALYSIS AND FORECASTING

During the twenties, a large number of writers on economic subjects were concerned primarily with answering the question, "How is business?" In order to give their answers precise meaning and to decide whether the economy was entering a new cyclical phase, or to predict when a new turning point was likely to occur, many business analysts relied heavily on formal statistical analysis of the past behavior of significant economic time series. Watching the current behavior of such indicators and making use of the observed leads became a main concern of business analysts. Business analysts and forecasters were stimulated in their work by the contributions of some leading academic economists, including the group of the Harvard Economic Service, and were encouraged by the apparently insatiable appetite of the general public for business forecasts. It was not until the failure of the forecasting fraternity to anticipate the Great Depression that the public became skeptical. But even in subsequent years many forecasters—particularly those who had shifted their attention more specifically to the stock market—continued to experiment with business barometers.

It is not surprising that in the decade when "forecasting the business cycle" had come to be regarded as a signal American

---

[9] Edwin Frickey, *Economic Fluctuations in the United States*, p. 13. A technical description of these series may be found in his Appendix XII-A. Frickey's interest in clearings goes back to the time of his association with the Harvard Economic Committee, when he developed the series on outside clearings used extensively in his book "to represent the volume of check transactions." See his "Bank Clearings Outside New York City, 1875-1914," *Review of Economic Statistics*, October 1925, pp. 252-62, and "A Statistical Study of Bank Clearings, 1875-1914," *Review of Economic Statistics*, May and August 1930, pp. 90-99 and 112-38.

[10] *Ibid.*, pp. 189-94.

contribution to the development of the social sciences, clearings and debits found numerous applications both as single-variable indicators of business conditions and as components of business barometers. The availability of the two series on a weekly basis, practically without delay, enhanced their usefulness for current economic analysis and forecasting.[11] The mere enumeration of the various barometers and indexes in which clearings or debits were used would require considerable space; the present section will be focused on two major contributions.

The view—one is tempted to say the doctrine—that clearings and debits are good, and reliable, indicators of business conditions was well established in the early twenties.[12] The extent to which this view was shared by Federal Reserve officials is indicated by the fact that bank debits were referred to as "the Board's statistics of volume of business."[13] Even now, when more and better monetary and other economic data have become available to the general public through the efforts of various public and private agencies, clearings and debits series still occupy a place of prominence.[14]

Snyder. Carl Snyder and the Harvard Economic Service, under the leadership of Warren Persons, may share the claim for having elevated clearings and debits to the position which they have come to occupy in business analysis and forecasting. Carl Snyder was one of the pioneers of the now rapidly growing group of business economists. While he wrote extensively on monetary problems and on the growth and fluctuations of the American economy since the Civil War, Snyder viewed his historical business cycle research largely as the foundation for analyzing current business conditions and prospects. Clearings and debits statistics ranked high among the raw

---

[11] For an attempt through the use of clearings series to anticipate the duration of the post-1929 contraction, see Joseph B. Hubbard, "Business Volumes during Periods of Decline and Recovery," *Review of Economic Statistics*, November 1930, pp. 181-85. For the use of clearings and five other series to measure and compare the amplitude of business cycles, see A. Ross Eckler, "A Measure of the Severity of Depressions, 1873-1932," *Review of Economic Statistics*, May 1933, pp. 75-81.

[12] Almost any contemporary text book on economic policy, business cycles, or monetary economics conveys this impression. See, for instance, H. P. Willis, *The Theory and Practice of Central Banking*, p. 343. See also Walter E. Spahr, *The Clearing and Collection of Checks*, Chap. XII, and the literature covering the early twenties quoted therein.

[13] See, for instance, *Federal Reserve Bulletin* for January 1922, p. 105 and February 1922, p. 243, note. For a more qualified answer to the question "What is the significance of debits to individual accounts as a business index?" see *Bulletin* for March 1941, p. 211.

[14] While considerable publicity is still given to clearings in the *Commercial and Financial Chronicle*, *Dun's Statistical Review*, and in the daily press (such as *New York Times, New York Herald Tribune, Wall Street Journal*, and numerous newspapers throughout the country), the national debits series is even more widely reproduced in its original form or reduced to indexes—with or without seasonal and other adjustments.

materials he exploited and refined in the development of adequate tools for the determination of economic policy.

The first of Snyder's two widely known measures of business conditions based on transactions series was the index of deposit turnover derived from the series discussed in the preceding chapter. This index, although further developed in subsequent years, was originally intended (when first presented in 1923) as an independent check on Snyder's index of the volume of trade.[15] The second measure—the clearings index of business—was derived from outside clearings by deflating them by a composite index of prices of the goods and services that give rise to check transactions; this price index was empirically weighted to produce a deflated series corresponding (after elimination of trend) as closely as possible to the index of the volume of trade for the years 1919 to 1923.[16] It was Snyder's belief "that bank clearings, or, as we now say, bank debits corrected by such an index of the general price level, are an accurate measure of the changes in trade and of what, following Mitchell, we have come to call the 'business cycle'."[17] For the years prior to 1919, clearings were substituted for debits through raising them to the level of outside debits by multiplying outside clearings by the average ratio they bore to debits from 1919 to 1922 (1.14).

The clearings index of business was originally based on the series for all reporting centers. The index was expressed as a percentage of a trend with a declining rate of growth, adjusted for seasonal variations and smoothed by a three-month moving average.[18] The increasing scope of the clearings series, which encompassed a steadily growing number of reporting centers, partly accounted for the higher rate of increase in the trend between 1875 and 1900. After 1900, the number of clearing houses was more stable. All additions involved the smaller communities. The average rate of increase of 3.5 per cent per annum was found to be consistent with the results

---

[15] "A New Index of the Volume of Trade," *Journal of the American Statistical Association,* December 1923, pp. 949-63.

[16] For details see Carl Snyder, "A New Clearings Index of Business for Fifty Years," *Journal of the American Statistical Association,* September 1924, pp. 329-35, and *Business Cycles and Business Measurements,* Chap. VI. The latter reference contains a tabulation of monthly data for March 1875-April 1926 on pp. 292-93, and a comparison of this price index with the A. T. and T. index, the Persons' index of trade, and several selected physical series (Chap. VIII, including charts 43 to 47).

[17] "New Measures in the Equation of Exchange," *American Economic Review,* December 1924, p. 699.

[18] The formula used was $\log Y = a + bX^{1/2} + cX$ (X = time, Y = clearings). In a subsequent revision, Snyder substituted Macaulay's series for that for all reporting outside centers.

obtained by investigators who worked with data relating to the physical growth of production.

Harvard Economic Service. While Snyder's clearings index of business, which was widely used during the twenties, is probably the best-known example of a single-variable index of business, the barometer of general business conditions which attracted worldwide attention also leaned heavily on clearings and debits. To review critically the fate of the Harvard index of general business conditions and to appraise its contribution to the development of forecasting technique—a task already undertaken by several writers—would fall beyond the scope of the present study. Here the purpose is merely to trace the use made of clearings and debits statistics in the Harvard index.

The purpose of the Harvard barometer was stated unambiguously by Persons in the first issue of the *Review of Economic Statistics:* "It is possible to measure general business prosperity and depression. Further, it is possible to ascertain the sequence of the phenomena— speculation, physical production, failures, prices, interest rate—of the business cycle."[19] The Harvard barometer was based on the comparative timing of three curves: A—speculation, B—business, and C—money. Clearings (and later debits) entered into two of these curves. New York City clearings, which represented speculation (along with the average price of 20 industrial stocks, the average price of 20 railroad stocks, the average yield on 10 railroad bonds, the number of shares sold on the New York Stock Exchange, and the value of building permits issued for 20 leading cities) in the original A curve, were dropped in 1927 when the make-up of this curve was changed. Clearings outside New York City, replaced in May 1923 by outside debits, on the other hand, were a component of the original B curve (industrial activity), which was supposed to reflect "the most fundamental business conditions."[20]

In the use of outside debits in their B curve, the Harvard Economic Service encountered two major difficulties which were shared by many other analysts and agencies making use of debits (and

---

[19] *Review of Economic Statistics,* April 1919, p. 111.

[20] In addition the B curve included Bradstreet's index of commodity prices, Bradstreet's number of business failures, the value of imports of merchandise into the United States, the tonnage of pig iron produced, and unfilled orders of the U.S. Steel Corporation. See *Review of Economic Statistics, Monthly Supplement,* July 1919, pp. 2-3.

clearings) statistics for forecasting purposes. One was rooted in the tendency of debits—at least in the larger financial centers included in the "outside" series—to be markedly affected by speculative transactions. The solution adopted was to eliminate the centers that registered most obviously the influence of stock exchange transactions and to broaden the series by adding a large number of centers for which data had become available but which accounted for only a relatively small dollar total.

When the volume of debits in the principal financial centers outside New York City began to be affected to a considerable degree by stock market and other speculative activities, the Harvard Economic Service eliminated seven financial centers from the outside debits series entering into the *B* curve.[21] The centers eliminated accounted in 1924-26 for approximately half of aggregate debits in all 140 centers outside New York City.

After the stock market crash of October 1929, however, the volume of debits arising from stock market activity in total debits dropped generally. When two years later the Harvard Economic Service undertook a general revision of its outside debits series, "two questions immediately arose: first, whether any of the seven centers previously removed should be restored; and, second, whether the debits curve could be improved by taking out any of the 133 centers now included."[22] After careful examination of the pertinent series for each of the seven cities previously dropped, a negative decision on the first issue was reached. Debits for an additional group of the 30 large centers were examined and it was found that, while the effects of speculative activity in 1928-29 could be "clearly traced in the fluctuation of the monthly figures" for these centers, "any serious attempt at complete elimination of the influence of stock trading would have involved the dropping of so many centers as to raise grave doubts with respect to the adequacy of the sample from the point of view of geographical and industrial distribution. The final decision, therefore, was to retain in the aggregate debits series all of

---

21 Boston, Philadelphia, Cleveland, Detroit, Chicago, San Francisco, and Los Angeles. See *Review of Economic Statistics*, November 1928, pp. 205-08. Some indications were found "that the speculative factor might also be significantly large in certain other centers, notably Cincinnati and St. Louis; but, after careful consideration of these doubtful cases, we decided that they could not be responsible for any significant portion of the observed speculative factor in outside debits." The 140 cities series continued to be used for the earlier period.

22 Edwin Frickey, "Outside Bank Debits Corrected for Seasonal Variation: Monthly and Weekly, 1919-31," *Review of Economic Statistics*, May 1931, pp. 76-84.

the 133 centers at present included." Subsequently (in January 1932) the outside debits series was enlarged by the inclusion of 108 additional (mostly small) centers.[23]

By the time this last revision of the outside debits series was made, all other components had been eliminated, for one reason or another, from the *B* curve, which from 1932 on became identical with the outside debits series. Thus, after several adjustments, the debits series at least survived until the attempt to forecast business conditions with the help of the three-curve barometer was given up altogether by the Harvard Economic Service (the publication of the three-curve barometer was discontinued in 1941), while several other series originally making up the *B* curve were gradually eliminated because they failed to conform to the pattern of cyclical behavior which they were expected to display on the basis of their business cycle conformity prior to World War I.

The other difficulty involving clearings and debits encountered by the Harvard Economic Service was largely statistical and was never solved satisfactorily. Monthly debits (and to an even greater degree weekly debits) are affected by the number of Sundays and holidays falling in a month. Also, since (prior to 1942) debits were reported weekly, the computation of monthly averages involved troublesome problems of allocating weeks which extended from one month to another. Originally the seasonal pattern derived for clearings outside New York City for the prewar (1903-16) period was applied after making adjustments to eliminate extreme values on tax payment dates. In April 1925 a new seasonal pattern was derived from the debits series itself,[24] and in the following year the statistical adjustments were refined by removing irregularities resulting from the occurrence of five Sundays in a given month and of the occurrence of Election Day as a legal holiday and of leap year.[25]

The successive revisions of the seasonal adjustment techniques developed by the Harvard Economic Service for monthly and weekly data (involving in the latter case determination of a "primary" and

---

[23] Debits for these centers had been collected by the Board of Governors continuously from May 1922 on. See *Review of Economic Statistics*, May 1932, pp. 80-87.

[24] *Ibid.*, January 1925, p. 18.

[25] *Ibid.*, April 1926, pp. 66-67. The Harvard Economic Service held such special adjustments of actual data preferable to estimating the number of working days by allowing for holidays since these vary in the different States and their effect is difficult to estimate. It was pointed out that as long as there is no change in the holidays observed, their influence is constant. This is subject to limitations because of the shifting date of Easter.

of a "secondary" seasonal movement) testify to the numerous troublesome difficulties encountered.[26] One of the major difficulties was the uncertainty with respect to the way in which holiday closing of banks actually affected the volume of debits on preceding and successive days. Another was the lack of uniformity in the observance of holidays and in banking practices throughout the country and, even more, the lack of precise knowledge of such observances and practices, particularly in the earlier years.

The example of the Harvard Economic Service was followed by the numerous private business advisory and forecasting services which mushroomed during the New Era. Thus, Babson's business value index—used to measure over-all business activity on the "Babsonchart"—was a variegated composite, of which debits was but one of 12 components.[27] Clearings (and later debits) outside New York City were used in index number form as the basis for the estimated "normal" of this composite because "bank clearings have formed the most reliable index of the net growth of the country's business in terms of dollars. They have the advantage of representing both the effect of price changes and of changes in the actual volume of business."

Other business and forecasting services have made and are still making similar use of debits statistics in graphic or index form, while still others content themselves with the presentation of the actual clearings and debits figures.

Carl Snyder's various indexes, as well as the Harvard barometer and several other forecasting devices drawing heavily on debits, which were developed during the twenties, were widely used to substantiate the optimistic claims of the New Era. Carl Snyder himself thought that his clearings index of business suggested "that depressions are lessening in severity."[28] In support of this hypothesis, he did not offer more evidence than the fact that the troughs of 1908 and 1914 were not quite so much below the theoretical "normal" as those in 1884 and 1894, and that while the earlier depressions ex-

---

[26] William L. Crum, "Weekly Fluctuations in Outside Bank Debits," *Review of Economic Statistics*, January 1927, pp. 30-36. The staffs of the Federal Reserve Bank of New York and of the Board of Governors at various times made studies with the purpose of improving the allocation of split weeks between consecutive months.

[27] Charles O. Hardy and Garfield V. Cox, *Forecasting Business Conditions*, pp. 43-49.

[28] *Business Cycles and Business Measurements*, p. 143.

tended over years, the more recent ones lasted for months only. In various articles during the late twenties, however, Snyder placed a great deal of emphasis on the recurrent nature of depressions and on the likelihood that the current boom would yield a new severe contraction. Consequently, when the storm broke, he belonged to the minority who could say "I told you so." But even the severity of the depression could not destroy Snyder's faith in the existence of a strong tendency for the American economy to grow at a constant rate, derived basically from deflated clearings.[29]

Snyder's endeavor to obtain physical rather than monetary measurements whenever these were available preserved him from an unhistorical approach to the appraisal of conditions as they developed during the late twenties. Those analysts who relied on debits more heavily than he did became an easy prey of statistical pitfalls. The root of the trouble—as far as statistics go—was the growing sensitivity of outside debits to purely speculative transactions. The difficulties of the Harvard index with the B curve, paired with the stubborn refusal of its sponsors to seek a substitute for debits that would represent more directly the physical volume of business activity, have been mentioned already.[30] Debits traceable to speculation in stocks, real estate, and commodities were mistakenly regarded by contemporary analysts as representing payments originating in the production and distribution of goods and services. The ever rising curve of debits was in consonance with the dominant mood of the New Era.

REGIONAL BUSINESS ANALYSIS

Prior to World War I, clearings were the only current statistical series published regularly for a large number of individual cities. They were widely used for comparing business trends in different parts of the country. In particular, the *Commercial and Financial Chronicle*, which grouped clearings for individual cities by broad geographic regions (and later by Federal Reserve districts), rather regularly commented on interregional differences in changes in the volume of

---

[29] For Snyder's views on the monetary implications of the constant rate of growth of the economy, see the following chapter.

[30] Indexes of industrial production were already available at that time, the first Federal Reserve index having appeared as early as March 1922 (see *Federal Reserve Bulletin*, March 1922, pp. 292-96). But since the Harvard index was based on the comparative study of the behavior during 1904-13 of the series underlying the three curves, the nonavailability of monthly production indexes for this early period must be presumed to be the explanation for the desperate effort to preserve debits as *the* indicator of business.

clearings and endeavored to explain such variations in terms of economic developments which affected some parts of the country more than others.

In spite of the great progress made since World War I in gathering and releasing economic data, analysts interested in business developments in specific areas are usually confronted with a discouraging dearth of relevant statistical data. Most of the important production and consumption series are available by short-time units only on a nationwide basis. Local payroll data are available in only a few States. Monthly sales of electric power are generally available only for the larger cities. The number of cities for which the Federal Reserve System releases department store sales data is considerably smaller than the list of centers for which debits are available. None of these types of local time series, moreover, possesses the same degree of uniformity in coverage, continuity, and comparability as debits. It is therefore obvious that in most cases local debits data are the main, if not the only, long-run economic series upon which the analyst of local business conditions can draw for historical comparisons.[31]

Since in most centers banks reporting debits account for 90 per cent or more of total deposits of the city's commercial banks, it is not surprising that debits have come to be regarded as the best available index of local or regional business conditions. They are used extensively (and in some cases—misused) by local trade and development associations, such as chambers of commerce and State, regional, and local planning agencies, by market analysts, banks, and others. Many local newspapers and publications of business associations of local and Statewide scope, as well as bulletins published by university bureaus of business research and by State commerce departments and similar agencies, carry local debits statistics. In most cases debits data are published by newspapers and various business and trade periodicals without analytical comments, although considerable special use is sometimes made of the data. Several State universities collect and publish debits for numerous smaller centers

[31] See, for instance, tabulations of debits by States and Census geographic regions in U.S. Department of Commerce, *State, Regional and Local Market Indicators, 1939–46* and *County and City Date Book, 1956.* During the twenties and the thirties, the Standard Statistical Service published regularly in its *Sales and Credit Prospects* seasonally adjusted indexes of bank debits for a large number of individual cities. These indexes were discontinued in 1942.

which do not report to the Federal Reserve System. Debits for additional centers are in some cases also collected and published by banks and chambers of commerce.

The wide, and in some cases, exclusive use of debits for the analysis of business conditions in a regional or local framework is not a matter of deliberate choice, but essentially reflects the lack of alternative or even of supplementary or corroborating material. The extent to which the limitation of debits as a tool of analysis is realized varies, but in general the reliance placed on debits is far greater than knowledge of the nature and make-up of these data would justify.

In analyses of economic fluctuations in a regional framework, debits were seized upon as an important body of statistical evidence readily available. The earliest elaborate statistical study in this field was made under the auspices of the Harvard Economic Service.[32] Ada M. Matthews and A. Ross Eckler found that "although bank debits for the various Federal Reserve districts agree quite closely in respect to their cyclical fluctuations, the same degree of similarity does not exist among their typical seasonal movements or among their trends." Matthews and Eckler discussed interdistrict differences in seasonal and cyclical patterns and in the trends in terms of economic developments within each district.

Philip Neff and Annette Weifenbach used bank debits, together with industrial employment, department store sales, and electric power sales to study timing and duration of economic fluctuations in six selected large centers (Chicago, Cleveland, Detroit, Los Angeles, Pittsburgh, and San Francisco).[33] F. L. Kidner drew heavily on debits in his study *California Business Cycles*.[34] Debits are the main body of statistical data drawn upon by Rutledge Vining in his statistical study "Regional Variation in Cyclical Fluctuations Viewed as a Frequency Distribution."[35] Debits have been utilized in practically all attempts made to present current regional indexes of business conditions.

---

[32] "Regional Business Conditions: A Study of Bank Debits," *Review of Economic Statistics*, August 1928, pp. 140-55.

[33] *Business Cycles in Selected Industrial Areas*. See also *American Economic Review, Proceedings*, March 1949, pp. 105-19.

[34] See, in particular, his index of bank debits in 15 California cities, and Figures 8(d), 9, 10, and 11(e).

[35] *Econometrica*, July 1945, pp. 183-219. See also *American Economic Review, Proceedings*, March 1949, pp. 89-104.

IX. Use of Velocity Indexes in Monetary Theory

Reformulation of the quantity theory of money around the turn of the century stimulated statistical studies in which data on deposit velocity were widely used. The special studies undertaken by the Comptroller of the Currency and later by the National Monetary Commission to accumulate empirical knowledge on the use of credit instruments were eagerly seized upon in order to estimate the volume of check payments (the product term $M'V'$).[1] Subsequently, the velocity of deposits (V') was estimated separately by deriving from banking statistics a series on total bank deposits. After the formation of the Federal Reserve System, publication of more comprehensive deposit statistics and of debits permitted estimates of total check payments and of the velocity of circulation of check money to be placed on a much firmer basis.

The literature on the quantity theory is extensive, and still growing.[2] This chapter is devoted to the statistical work undertaken by both proponents and critics of the theory, which constitutes one of the first and outstanding attempts to build economic theory on empirical data. As Marget rightly points out, "a considerable number of those who denied any validity to the concept of 'velocity' have based their argument upon the supposed impossibility of measuring it statistically. It is, however, characteristic that the writers concerned should not have bothered to take account of the measures of 'velocity' provided by writers such as Fisher, Snyder, Burgess, and others, to say nothing of bothering to develop an argument designed to show why the work of these writers cannot be improved upon."[3] In this chapter attention will be confined to tracing the use of clearings and

---

[1] The following symbols and definitions are used throughout this chapter:

M = amount of currency
M' = amount of bank deposits
V = velocity of currency
V' = velocity of bank deposits

P = price level
T = volume of trade
$MV + M'V' = PT$

These are the notations introduced by Fisher and accepted by most writers on the subject, although at times Kemmerer, Snyder, and other writers used different symbols.

[2] For a comprehensive review of the literature, see Hugo Hegeland, *The Quantity Theory of Money.*

[3] Arthur W. Marget, *The Theory of Prices,* p. 295, footnote 14.

of debits statistics in estimating the volume of check payments and the velocity of circulation of deposits. Only the statistical, not the theoretical, side of the controversy raised by the vigorous proponents of the quantity theory will be dealt with, and time series other than those which are the subject of this study will be mentioned only in passing.

Kemmerer. In his pioneering attempt (in his dissertation originally submitted in 1903 and published in revised form in 1907) to test empirically the quantity theory of money, Professor Kemmerer used bank clearings to estimate total check circulation $(M'V')$.[4] In order to raise the reported volume of checks cleared to the volume of checks written, he took as a point of departure the very fragmentary data which had become available as a result of the Comptroller of the Currency's investigations into the use of deposit currency conducted in 1896 under the direction of Professor David Kinley. After making an estimate of the total volume of check payments for that year and raising it by one-third to allow for currency payments (MV), Kemmerer proceeded to construct an annual series of the volume of combined check and currency payments since 1870. The $M'V'$ series was based on the assumption that "35 per cent of the country's total check circulation passed through the clearing houses each year of that period," a proportion that Kemmerer derived by averaging the ratios of total clearings to the estimated $M'V'$ for 1896 and 1891 (the latter derived from Willard Fisher's estimates).[5] Total check circulation was thus obtained by multiplying, for each fiscal year ending June 30, total reported United States clearings by a constant factor 100/35.

Kemmerer's "verification" of the equation of exchange consisted of a comparison of the actual fluctuations in the price level with a theoretical price level (P = "relative circulation") derived from the remaining members of the equation of exchange

$$\left(P = \frac{MV + M'V'}{T}\right).$$

---

[4] Edwin W. Kemmerer, *Money and Credit Instruments in Their Relation to General Prices.* For an early critical evaluation of Kemmerer's analysis, see Warren M. Persons, "Quantity Theory as Tested by Kemmerer," *Quarterly Journal of Economics,* February 1908.

[5] Willard Fisher, "Money and Credit Paper in the Modern Market," *Journal of Political Economy,* September 1895, pp. 391-413.

In the short concluding chapter Kemmerer relied on the visual evidence for 1879-1908 presented in a chart which "tells its own story. The general movement of the two curves taken as a whole is the same, while the individual variations from year to year exhibit a striking similarity."

The increasing divergency between the theoretical price level (which rose rather continuously from the late eighties through the first decade of the twentieth century) and the actual price level, which, in terms of Kemmerer's series, at the end of the period amounted to about 20 per cent, did not disturb Kemmerer and was not commented upon. Three minor divergencies between actual prices and the "relative circulation" were noted, but otherwise the evidence presented was considered conclusive.[6]

Actually, the parallelism between the theoretical and the actual price level (as measured by the "general index of prices and wages" constructed by Kemmerer) might have been closer, since the divergence of the two curves was largely due to a spurious adjustment in clearings figures made by Kemmerer (described in his explanatory note to the table of monetary and check circulation) and, apparently, not detected by the numerous users and critics of his estimates. For the years prior to May 17, 1892, Kemmerer subtracted the estimated volume of exchanges resulting from New York stock sales from total clearings, claiming that clearing of payments arising from stock trading was removed from the New York Clearing House exchanges by the activities of the New York Stock Clearing House that began to operate on that date. This was not correct, as only a relatively small number of the most active stocks were so cleared (originally only four stocks); balances arising from the clearing of each individual stock continued to pass through the Clearing House, as did all transactions for stocks and bonds not cleared by the facilities of the Stock Exchange Clearing House. Kemmerer consequently made an erroneous adjustment for the fiscal years 1879 to 1891 which reduced the volume of total United States check circulation by $20

---

[6] Kemmerer, *Money and Credit Instruments in Their Relation to General Prices*, p. 150. Irving Fisher's attempt to improve Kemmerer's comparison by substituting a smaller estimate of the velocity of circulation of currency (see Figure 12 in Fisher's book for this modification of Kemmerer's Chart IV) did not produce a strikingly better parallelism, but Fisher remarked that "when minute comparison is made the selection of 18 as the estimate of velocity gives a slightly better agreement between the two curves than does 47." *The Purchasing Power of Money*, p. 278.

billion to $60 billion a year. Since in the base years the numerator is thus underestimated by 24 per cent, the growth of the index of total monetary circulation is considerably exaggerated. Actually, by recomputing Kemmerer's index to include all reported clearings, the "relative circulation" for 1908 becomes 100 instead of 132, which is much closer to the actual P of 103. The "relative circulation" is correspondingly reduced for almost all other years.

Kemmerer's doctoral dissertation is the best known early instance, in this country at least, in which a theoretical exposition of monetary economics was followed by a statistical verification. It is not necessary to enumerate here the countless limitations of the material on which Kemmerer built up the statistical part of his study and to dwell upon the inadequacy of the assumptions made. In spite of its statistical limitations, Professor Kemmerer's book opened a new chapter in monetary analysis.

Since Kemmerer's groundbreaking attempt to test the quantity theory of money, all subsequent investigations in the same direction have endeavored to obtain better time series for all the variables entering the equation of exchange. Persistent efforts in this direction, in particular by Irving Fisher and Carl Snyder, have resulted in a considerable enrichment of our empirical knowledge of the growth of production, the money supply, and price fluctuations. Numerous time series of the volume of production, the volume of money flows, and the stock of money have been derived from the data so accumulated, and ingenious indexes have been devised for testing the various versions of the quantity theory of money. Many empirical investigations which grew out of efforts to verify the equation of exchange have contributed greatly to the number of economic time series that became available during the second and third decades of this century. They have also considerably stimulated the development of statistical techniques, particularly in the field of index numbers.

Fisher. Several years after Kemmerer's study was published, Irving Fisher reformulated the equation of exchange into the form in which it has become widely used in monetary analysis. His test followed very closely the one made by Kemmerer and involved use of clearings for estimating $M'V'$. Fisher compared for 1896-1909 an index of the price level derived from $\dfrac{MV + M'V'}{T}$ with an "index of general prices" derived by combining the Bureau of Labor Statistics index of wholesale prices with series on wages and security prices. His two curves ran roughly parallel but nevertheless showed rather large deviations in some years. Fisher satisfied himself on the closeness of agreement of the two curves by comparing their directions of change (in 3 out of 12 years they moved in different directions), and by computing a coefficient of correlation (which was found to be 0.97 and, according to Fisher, "overstates the parallelism"). Making certain assumptions as to the probable error involved in estimating the six magnitudes involved (2 to 3 per cent for M and M', 5 to 10 per cent for V, V', P, and T), Fisher then proceeded to adjust various series in proportion to the probable error in order to obtain consistency among the terms of the equation.

Fisher went so far as to conclude that "to those who have faith in the *a priori* proof of the equation of exchange the real significance of the remarkable agreement in our statistical results should be understood as a confirmation, not of the equation by the figures, but of the figures by the equation. There are discrepancies in our inductive verification; but these are all well within the limit of errors of measurement. The discrepancies prove that slight errors exist among the figures; otherwise, they would conform exactly to the relation prescribed by the equation of exchange."[7]

Anderson. A most searching analysis of Kemmerer's and Fisher's statistical investigations, which "reach a high-water mark in the effort to give statistical demonstrations of the quantity theory," was furnished in 1917 by B. M. Anderson, an inveterate critic of the quantity theory of money.[8] The resulting controversy (including Fisher's rebuttals) shed (mainly because of Anderson's diligent search for relevant though fragmentary data and because of his inquiries with bankers, brokers, supervisory authorities, and others conversant with monetary practices and custom) considerable light on the shortcomings of clearings statistics as a measure of the flow of check payments, thus supporting the movement then under way (see Chapter III) to supplant clearings by debits statistics.

Anderson's criticism was focused on Fisher's contribution which,

---

[7] *The Purchasing Power of Money*, p. 298.
[8] *The Value of Money*, in particular Chap. XIX.

being the more recent and the more substantial, had attracted wide attention. Anderson did not question in any important way Fisher's figures for M and M', "the results of fairly simple computations based on governmental statistics," and concentrated first on the estimate of $M'V'$ for 1909. He charged that Fisher committed a triple error in deriving that magnitude from Professor Kinley's data because: (1) his assumption that the volume of checks used in trade is the same as total check circulation was not tenable (actually, a large volume of checks arises from loans and repayments, tax payments, gifts, etc., and should be deducted from estimated total check circulation); (2) corrections of outside New York City data, made by Fisher on the assumption that the day for which data on check deposits were available was an abnormal one, were not justified; and (3) check transactions in New York were grossly underestimated, since, for instance, the returns of private banks and of trust companies were not complete.

Since some of Fisher's errors were compensating, Anderson accepted Fisher's total estimate of check deposits for 1909. He held, however, that (1) check deposits are not an adequate measure of $M'V'$ and (2) that by assigning to New York clearings the weight of one against five for outside clearings to obtain an interpolator for his series, Fisher reduced its cyclical fluctuations. Anderson showed that, contrary to Fisher's assumption, New York deposits were underestimated rather than overestimated by the use of clearings, while the undercount assumed for the rest of the country was exaggerated.

So much for the criticism of the statistical basis of Fisher's work and for the methods used by him (and by Kemmerer) to estimate $M'V'$. Anderson's other major criticism was directed against the assumption that the right-hand side of the equation represents "trade" (at current prices). He rightly stressed that numerous types of payments (those related to the current flow of goods and services as well as those which are not) other than trade transactions were made with check money. This Fisher did not contest, but claimed that some types of trade transactions were not reflected by checks, so that much of the overcounting in one place was offset by undercounting in another.[9] Anderson tried to invalidate this contention by

---

[9] See his discussion with Anderson in *The Annalist* (various issues between Feb. 17 and Mar. 20, 1916).

a minute examination of the obviation of check payments by arrangements for clearing transactions at the New York Stock Exchange and the Chicago Board of Trade (the biggest security and commodity markets in the country) and by other procedures.

Burns. Events after the end of World War I confirmed Anderson in his belief that the quantity theory was "crushed by the weight of facts."[10] He again followed Fisher's method in testing the hypothetical price level derived from the equation of exchange against the actual course of prices during the period 1919-28. A. F. Burns, by dissecting Anderson's statistical method, removed the foundation for Anderson's claim that in 1928 "prices would have to be 83 per cent higher than they are, if the quantity theory of money were true."[11] Burns showed that by using inappropriate time series, in particular wholesale prices as a measure of P (although Fisher's model clearly involved an index of the general price level), and by neglecting to use the most reliable estimates for M, M', and V', Anderson arrived at conclusions at variance with those reached when the best available data were used. Indeed, even using Anderson's index of physical volume of trade (T) and accepting his contention that V was stable (as well as the weights 9 and 1 for $M'V'$ and MV, respectively), Burns reduced the maximum deviation in 1928 between hypothetical and actual P from 82.5 to 28.7 per cent. When substituting Copeland's T for Anderson's, the agreement between the hypothetical and actual price levels was even more striking, the difference in no single year through 1927 (the terminal year of Copeland's series) exceeding 7 per cent.[12]

Snyder. Anderson's attack was intended not merely to destroy a defective analytical tool, but to cast disrepute on what was advocated as a guide for economic policy. The target of Anderson's criticism was, among others, Carl Snyder, who proposed a simplified version of the equation of exchange and whose policy recommendations were based on a reformulation of the quantity theory of money.

Snyder's version of the equation of exchange was based on three

---

[10] "Commodity Price Stabilization a False Goal of Central Bank Policy," *Chase Economic Bulletin*, May 8, 1929, p. 12.

[11] "Quantity Theory and Price Stabilization," *American Economic Review*, December 1929, pp. 561-79.

[12] See footnote 18, p. 126. In addition to Burns' detailed criticism of Anderson's data, it should be noted that Anderson's computation of V' "by dividing total bank clearings of the country plus Federal Reserve clearings by deposits" (*Chase Economic Bulletin*, May 8, 1929, p. 23) involves duplications in the dividend, inasmuch as many checks that are recorded as bank clearings also enter into Federal Reserve clearings.

conclusions derived from a study of the elements of the equation with the help of several new indexes which he constructed:[13]

1. That velocity of deposits and volume of trade show cyclical fluctuations that are similar in timing and relative amplitude.

2. That the rate of secular increase in the volume of trade is constant.

3. That the velocity of circulating media has not undergone any clear secular change.

The first conclusion should be regarded as the main step in passing from Fisher's to Snyder's version of the equation of exchange. A study of the velocity of demand deposits for the five years after the armistice ("any other five or six more peaceful and less tumultuous years would yield a similar result") furnished Snyder with what he took to be conclusive proof that the variations in velocity of bank deposits were nearly synchronous with those in the volume of trade and that their ratio was a constant. "The inference seems clear that, under existing conditions in this country, the velocity of circulation is not normally an influential factor in the determination of the price level, though under other conditions, as in Germany in the last few years, velocity may be a very strong influence."[14] Lacking direct evidence on fluctuations in the velocity of currency, Snyder assumed that V' and V were "fairly synchronous." Furthermore, Willford I. King had found (for the period prior to 1920) that there was a fairly fixed ratio between the amount of currency in circulation and total demand deposits. Since volume of currency payments is small in relation to check transactions, Snyder, partly on the strength of King's findings, used $M'V'$ as an index of $M'V' + MV$.

Snyder's transformation of the equation of exchange may, then, be summarized as follows:

By decomposing T into the trend (T_t) and cyclical-accidental (T_c) components, and substituting $M'V'$ for $M'V' + MV$, Fisher's

---

[13] "New Measures in the Equation of Exchange," *American Economic Review*, December 1924, pp. 699-713.

During his long career as the general statistician of the Federal Reserve Bank of New York, Carl Snyder devoted much effort to the improvement and refinement of indexes of the volume of trade and of the general price level, using additional material that was not available to earlier investigators. As a measure of $M'V'$ he used the product of demand deposits at weekly reporting member banks (another series developed by him) and an index of deposit velocity described in Chap. VII, rather than clearings.

[14] For a claim that Snyder's theory does not fit the British statistics, see Arthur C. Pigou, *Industrial Fluctuations*, pp. 147-50. See also Willford I. King, "Recent Monetary Experiments and Their Effect upon the Theory of Money and Prices," *Journal of the American Statistical Association*, June 1935, pp. 387-400.

equation of exchange becomes: $M'V' = PT_iT_c$. But since $V'/T_c = K$ (a constant), the equation can be written $M'K = PT_i$, where $T_i = ab^n$ (b being estimated by Snyder at 3½ and in subsequent publications at 4 per cent). Hence $M' = PT_i/K$ and $P = KM'/T_i$.

This simplified version of the equation of exchange was first suggested in 1924.[15] Snyder presented, for 1890-1923, an estimate of the theoretical price level by dividing outside clearings by an index of industrial production (and only for the period since 1919 by an actual index of trade), corrected for trend. While proclaiming that "the movements of the general price level are no longer a mystery; and we now possess the data upon which to calculate what this price level will be, under given conditions," he concluded nevertheless on a note of caution: "The discrepancies shown, and the irregularities of the hypothetical line, indicate that an exact congruence seems not yet obtainable." Nor does the empirical material "settle the vexed question of causal relationships."

These cautious conclusions were later replaced by a very articulate monetary theory. A monetary policy which would increase the money supply at the rate of 4 per cent per annum (the estimated normal rate of growth of trade) would, in Snyder's view, stabilize the price level, as the effects of short-run fluctuations in business activity would be offset by synchronous fluctuations in the velocity of money of about the same amplitude (K thus remaining constant).[16] If M' increased at the same rate as T_i, the value of P determined by the equation $P = KM'/T_i$ would remain unchanged.

During the late twenties and thirties Snyder further developed the statistical underpinning of this theory and vigorously advocated its policy implications, first in unpublished memoranda and later in several articles presenting an essentially identical line of reasoning and factual material in chart form. Snyder's final version of the equation of exchange retained none of the variables that entered

---

[15] *American Economic Review*, December 1924, p. 710, in the form $P/K = M$, K being defined as the ratio of velocity of circulation to volume of trade expressed in terms of their deviations from trend. Snyder was the first to present a *monthly* chart (1919-23), thus inviting (although not actually providing) studies of lead-and-lag relationships.

[16] "New Measures of the Relations of Credit and Trade," *Proceedings of the Academy of Political Science*, January 1930, particularly p. 29. See also "Industrial Growth and Monetary Theory," *Economic Forum* (Summer, 1933), pp. 275-90, where the long-term rate of growth is estimated for 1918-33 at 4.3 per cent per annum.

Fisher's equation except P.[17] It did not involve the use of time series, with which the present study is concerned, although the theory on which it was based did.

Copeland. Major improvements in the statistical measurement of the elements of the equation of exchange are due to Morris A. Copeland, whose study was published a few months before the economic collapse of 1929.[18] Copeland derived an index of velocity of the *total* money supply ($M + M'$) by taking as a starting point his own estimates of total United States debits to individual accounts.[19] From these, he subtracted debits to time deposit accounts, estimated (following Burgess) at twice the size of time deposits. In order to estimate the total amount of "obligations discharged," he added to debits to demand deposit accounts (1) those to Federal Government accounts at Federal Reserve Banks and (2) the estimated amount of cash payments not already included (via currency withdrawals) in debits; this amount was estimated by multiplying half of the currency in circulation by the rate of turnover of demand deposits, assuming that half of all cash payments was made with money freshly withdrawn from deposit accounts and therefore already recorded as debits. Dividing this estimated volume of total payments by the sum of demand deposits increased by one-half of the currency in circulation, Copeland obtained a monthly index of velocity of the total money supply (on a working day basis) for 1919-27.

In a companion study Copeland used this index of velocity of the total money supply (as well as several other indexes developed in the earlier paper) to test empirically two conflicting hypotheses on the relationship between changes in the quantity of currency in circulation and general rises and falls of prices.[20] Copeland restated the equation of exchange as $MV = K(PT + R)$. In this equation, cash and check payments are combined, so that Copeland's MV is equivalent to Fisher's $MV + M'V'$. The right-hand side of the

---

[17] See *Proceedings* cited in the preceding footnote, and also "The Problem of Monetary and Economic Stability," *Quarterly Journal of Economics*, February 1935, pp. 173-205. For a brief critical discussion of Snyder's monetary theories, see Rollin G. Thomas, *Our Modern Banking and Monetary System* (second edition), pp. 492-96.

[18] "Special Purpose Indexes for the Equation of Exchange for the United States, 1919-27," *Journal of the American Statistical Association*, June 1929, pp. 109-22. Copeland also presented more refined estimates of M' as well as a broadened index of T designed to include financial and other types of transactions that are not intimately related to the volume of the current flow of goods and services.

[19] See Chap. III, pp. 36-37.

[20] "Money, Trade, and Prices—A Test of Causal Primacy," *Quarterly Journal of Economics*, August 1929, pp. 648-66.

equation is expanded to include transactions such as tax and premium payments, capital flotations and retirements, and other types of financial transactions which, although an important part of total payments, can by no stretch of imagination be considered to be a component of PT. These payments are measured by R.

The first of the hypotheses tested was formulated by Holbrook Working, who claimed causal primacy for M.[21] The second, contained in Mitchell's *Business Cycles*, identified P and T as the "active factors" most of the time in the equation of exchange.[22] The originality of Copeland's contribution was in testing the two alternative hypotheses by using monthly data to study the lead-and-lag relationship at turning points between the various time series involved. The test did not show that M was clearly leading P. The analysis of differences in the timing of the turning points of T and V led Copeland to conclude that Working's hypothesis with respect to their synchronization found no support in the data. On the other hand, Copeland found that the seasonal patterns of T, V, and M, as well as of $PT + R$ and MV, were consistent with Mitchell's hypothesis that most of the time $PT + R$ was the active side of the equation, except when MV had expanded up to the limit permitted by our monetary and banking system.

Keynes. Although review of the use of clearings and debits in foreign literature on monetary economics is beyond the scope of the present study, an exception should be made for Lord Keynes because of the general importance of his *Treatise on Money* and also because of the use he made of Carl Snyder's estimates and of American material in general. The part dealing with monetary factors and their fluctuations, "consists, in the main, of a statistical study of the monetary elements on the left-hand side of this equation [of exchange as reformulated by Keynes], as distinguished from what we have called the investment elements; and these purely monetary elements are

---

[21] "Prices and the Quantity of Circulating Medium, 1890-1921," *Quarterly Journal of Economics*, February 1923, pp. 228-56. Working suggested using the equation of exchange, as formulated by Fisher, to forecast prices without directly estimating V. Claiming that fluctuations of V and T are synchronous, although in opposite directions, he estimated the long-run values of the ratio V/T as the reciprocal M/P. The "normal" values of M/P are ordinates of a smooth curve fitted by the method of least squares to empirical values. The current value of M was then used to forecast P.

[22] Wesley C. Mitchell, *Business Cycles*, p. 137.

the same as, or similar to, those of which the traditional quantity equation takes account."[23]

At the danger that he might "appear to the reader to be reverting to the old-fashioned 'quantity of money' approach to the problem of price determination," Keynes indulged in a series of refinements in estimating the supply side of the equation. He rewrote the equation (which he held to be "an identity, a truism") as $M'V' = \pi\, O$. The right-hand term is the product of the volume of output and its price level. In the left-hand side, M' is the volume of "industrial circulation," while V' is compounded of the average velocity of several types of money and an element related to the balance between savings and investment. This equation was neither evaluated nor tested statistically. Instead, Keynes concentrated on the estimation of the velocities of two types of demand deposits (income and business deposits, as defined in Chapter 3 of the *Treatise*, Vol. I) which together represent the "active circulation"; the velocity of savings deposits was assumed to be zero. It is Keynes' estimates of the rates of turnover, rather than his definitions of numerous auxiliary magnitudes and symbols (of which he makes hardly any use subsequently), that are of interest to this study.

Since data on the ownership of demand deposits were not available for either England or the United States when Keynes wrote, actual estimates could be made for the average velocity of total demand deposits only; the further estimates of the variability of the rates of turnover of business deposits hinged on the validity of the assumption that Keynes' guess of the velocity of income deposits was realistic and that this velocity was relatively stable. Estimates of the velocity of business deposits for the two countries (for 1923 for the United States and 1926-28 for Great Britain) were obtained by assuming certain values for the velocity of income deposits. For Great Britain, Keynes estimated the velocity of demand deposits (for 1909, 1913, and 1920-29) as a ratio of total clearings to crudely ("on the basis of such information as I have been able to obtain from bankers") estimated current deposits. To make allowances for (1) debits not reflected in clearings and (2) the difference between the amount of year-end deposits (used in computations) and annual

---

[23] *Treatise on Money*, Vol. II, pp. 5-6.

average deposits, Keynes raised his estimates for 1924-29 by 43 per cent and arrived at annual turnover rates ranging from 57 to 63.[24] These rates were higher than the rough estimate of the velocity of business deposits in the United States, obtainable for 1923 from the early work of Snyder and Burgess.

Keynes' estimates of the velocity of circulation for England are clearly of a cruder nature than those made by Kemmerer and Fisher for total United States deposits a quarter of a century earlier. But whereas the American investigators attempted to derive time series in order to compare the actual fluctuations of the price level with those derived from the equation of exchange, Keynes was primarily interested in the order of magnitude involved.[25]

The studies reviewed briefly above are, of course, only a selective choice from a much wider body of similar empirical investiga ions without mentioning a voluminous critical literature. Gradually, however, the proponents of the quantity theory of money have shifted their ground. Clark Warburton, for instance, one of the best known contemporary proponents of the quantity theory of money in this country, while recognizing that "the ratio of bank debits to bank deposits is the most comprehensive measure available of the rate of use of money,"[26] measures the rate of use of money in terms of the ratio of expenditures of business and individuals for final products (rather than of total debits to individual accounts to cash balances). Warburton argues—finding considerable support for his position in the work by Morris Copeland on money flows—that variations in the ratio of debits to deposits reflect variations in the rate of use of money for payments associated with property transfers

---

[24] The publication of total debits for the British clearing banks was announced while Keynes' *Treatise* was in press.

[25] "The reasonable agreement of these figures [with those of Burgess and Snyder] is some slight confirmation that the *order of magnitude* of these guesses may be fairly accurate—which is all I claim for them" (*Treatise on Money*, Vol. II, p. 39). Keynes had remarked earlier: "Professor Fisher's guesses have turned out too high. Since my guesses for England are not much better based than were his for the United States 25 years ago, they may suffer from the same defect" (p. 35, note 1).

For attempts to show the validity of the Keynesian liquidity preference theory by correlating the velocity of deposits and the short-term interest rate, see M. Kalecki, "The Short-Term Rate of Interest and the Velocity of Cash Circulation," *Review of Economic Statistics*, May 1941, pp. 97-99, and *Studies in Economic Dynamics*, pp. 32-46; also James Tobin, "Liquidity Preference and Monetary Policy," *Review of Economic Statistics*, May 1947, pp. 124-31. For a detailed critique of Tobin's assumptions and findings, see Clark Warburton, "Money Velocity and Monetary Policy," *Review of Economic Statistics*, November 1948, pp. 304-14. See also J. N. Behrman, "The Short-Term Interest Rate and the Velocity of Circulation," *Econometrica*, April 1948, pp. 185-90.

[26] "The Volume of Money and the Price Level between the World Wars," *Journal of Political Economy*, June 1945, pp. 150-63. A similar statement appears in "The Secular Trend in Monetary Velocity," *Quarterly Journal of Economics*, February 1949, p. 70. See also, "Quantity and Frequency of Use of Money in the United States, 1919-45," *Journal of Political Economy*, October 1946, pp. 436-50.

and contracts of indebtedness far more than they reflect variations in the rate of use of money for payments associated with the production and marketing of goods and services. Warburton's numerous and elaborate studies on monetary velocity are, therefore, in terms of circular rather than of exchange velocity, and make no use of the type of data which are the subject of the present study. Similarly, Selden's recent study of velocity deals mainly with income velocity and examines no fewer than 38 different statistical series measuring it.[27]

Since changes in velocity are indicative of underlying changes in economic (and particularly in credit) conditions, the Federal Reserve System has at various times studied the possibilities of relating legal reserve requirements—one of the tools of credit policy—to changes in the velocity of bank deposits. These studies, conducted by the Federal Reserve System over a long period of time, have resulted in proposals to relate reserve requirements for member banks to deposit velocity. The proposal involving a graduation of reserve requirements according to the rate of use of deposits, made originally nearly 20 years ago, has re-emerged in recent years in a modified form.

The present system of reserve requirements, based essentially on the three-way classification of member banks according to their geographical location, was inherited from the National Banking Act.[28] Several alternative proposals to shift reserve requirements to a more rational basis consistent with modern views on the nature and functions of legal bank reserves have been made within and outside the Federal Reserve System ever since it was formed. In 1931, a special Committee on Bank Reserves of the Federal Reserve System undertook an elaborate study of the functions of legal reserves, of the reserve requirements then in existence, and of the behavior of various classes of deposits. The Committee, whose studies (directed by W. W. Riefler) involved extensive use of debits and other statistics, recommended a plan for determining required

---

[27] Richard T. Selden, "Monetary Velocity in the United States" in *Studies in the Quantity Theory of Money*, edited by Milton Friedman. See also Lawrence S. Ritter, "Income Velocity and Anti-Inflationary Monetary Policy," *American Economic Review*, March 1959, pp. 120-29.

[28] See "Reserve Requirements of Commercial Banks," *Bank Reserves—Some Major Factors Affecting Them* (Federal Reserve Bank of New York), p. 5.

reserves of member banks which would take into consideration the activity as well as the size of bank deposits.[29]

The proposal of the Riefler Committee, which became known as the "velocity reserve proposal," would have established uniform requirements for all classes of deposits, consisting of a 5 per cent basic reserve combined with an additional reserve equal to 50 per cent of the average daily debits to deposit accounts. It became the subject of a lively controversy in which critics as well as proponents of the velocity reserve proposal made wide use of debits data, including velocity estimates for individual cities and groups of cities.[30]

While the velocity proposal never reached Congress in the form of a bill, the matter was given further study within and outside the Federal Reserve System until the outbreak of World War II shifted attention to more vital issues.[31] After the war, a special research committee of the Federal Reserve System recommended that the present system of reserve determination be replaced by one which would involve different requirements for interbank deposits and all other deposits, thus abolishing the present grouping of member banks in three classes. These recommendations were presented in 1948 to Congressional committees, but were not endorsed officially by the Board of Governors.[32] While not involving direct measurement of deposit activity, they were to some extent a revival of the plan formulated nearly two decades ago, since the proposal for higher reserve requirements for interbank deposits than for all other types of deposits is motivated, at least partly, by their higher rates of turnover.

---

[29] *Member Bank Reserves*, Report of the Committee on Bank Reserves of the Federal Reserve System, 1931.

[30] See in particular B. M. Anderson, "Proposed Banking Legislation," *Chase Economic Bulletin*, Apr. 25, 1932, particularly pp. 30-35. Anderson's criticism was examined in a lengthy (confidential) memorandum of the Committee on Bank Reserves (*Member Bank Reserve Requirements*, October 1932) which drew a rejoinder from Anderson (also confidential and unpublished, dated Apr. 12, 1934); both documents contain considerable factual and analytical material on the seasonal and cyclical behavior of deposit velocity. Angell's objections to this proposal (aside from the general proposition that any move to restrict credit by exerting pressure on reserves may be counteracted by banks by increasing the volume of rediscounting) is summarized in the statement that "Exchange velocity appears to move with or after other important factors, not before them. The seeds of disturbance are therefore likely to have become too deeply imbedded for successful extirpation before action based on exchange velocity alone can become effective." *The Behavior of Money*, p. 126.

[31] See, however, *Annual Report of the Board of Governors of the Federal Reserve System*, 1932, pp. 260-85.

[32] *Hearings on Credit Policies before the Joint Committee on the Economic Report*, 80th Cong., 2d Sess., May 27, 1948, pp. 131-52; *Monetary, Credit and Fiscal Policies*, a collection of statements submitted to the subcommittee on Monetary, Credit and Fiscal Policies, 81st Cong., 1st Sess., p. 55; and *Report of the Subcommittee on Monetary, Credit and Fiscal Policy* (the Douglas Committee), 81st Cong., 2d Sess., pp. 32-37. See also "Proposed Revision of Reserve Requirements," *Federal Reserve Bulletin*, April 1958, pp. 427-29.

X. Concluding Remarks

In this study an attempt has been made to appraise the use of a body of statistical data in the light of a critical analysis of their history and make-up. It may be useful to summarize briefly findings with respect to the adequacy of clearings and debits for the various uses to which they have been put.

While debits are clearly superior to clearings as a measure of the volume of aggregate money payments, clearings are of historical interest because they are available for a period for which other economic time series are extremely scarce. As comprehensive bench-marks are not available, it is not possible to determine what pro-portion of aggregate money payments enters into clearings and whether this proportion has been subject to cyclical or long-run changes. Nor can it be estimated with any degree of reliability what proportion of clearings represents interbank payments, but it is likely that, in the short run at least, fluctuations in the amount of bank drafts cleared are closely associated with the amounts of business and personal checks cleared. It is also likely that any changes in the proportion of bank drafts and of checks in the total volume of clearings as well as in the proportion of money transactions giving rise to checks collected through local clearing arrangements have taken place only gradually. The numerous changes in collection procedures and in the membership of individual clearing house associations were only a minor influence, which did not obscure, on the whole, the cyclical movements of national aggregates.

It must also be kept in mind that when the earlier investigators used outside clearings for the purpose of analyzing cyclical fluctu-ations in the American economy, they turned to these data not because of their close relationship to gross national product—a statistical concept developed many years later—but because clearings were the only available direct indicator of aggregate payments. From the point of view of cyclical analysis, the essential fact is not that clearings cover a gradually increasing proportion of all monetary

132

transactions in the economy, but that, on balance, the volume of all types of transactions covered by clearings fluctuated positively and consistently with the business cycle. While before World War I rather systematic leads and lags existed at turning points, they were relatively so small that the dating of turning points of aggregate business based on the outside clearings series alone was capable of yielding a chronology of business cycles not much different from the one presently established on the basis of thorough study of a much broader body of statistical and other material.

The lead at troughs and the lag at the peaks of the outside clearings series reflected largely the fact that cyclical movements were superimposed on a strong upward trend. The trend curve, derived from the outside clearings series adjusted for price changes through an index of the general price level, has been taken by several investigators (such as Carl Snyder) to represent the growth of the physical volume of goods and services produced. Actually, the increase in outside clearings, particularly during the 50 years prior to World War I, reflects also the increased proportion of the national output which is sold rather than consumed by the producers themselves or exchanged for other goods and services without the use of money. Also, it is likely that the use of checks by individuals, particularly in the lower and middle income brackets, has been increasing gradually, so that the secular growth of clearings represents partly the substitution of payments by check for payments in currency or for payments in kind. Similarly—although definite evidence is not available—it appears that the increased importance of firms of national scope in production and in distribution has caused the aggregate amount of check payments per physical unit of final goods and services supplied to ultimate consumers to increase rather than to decrease. Finally, with the growing urbanization of the population (accompanied by large-scale real estate developments), and with the development of organized securities and commodity markets, the amount of checks reflecting speculative transactions was on the increase, at least through the twenties. Thus, more general use of checks and the increased contribution of financial transactions to the total amount of checks cleared account for part of the rising trend of clearings which cannot be taken to reflect (after proper adjustment for price changes) the growth of physical volume of production alone.

If it had been possible to eliminate from clearings the amount traceable directly to financial transactions, the trend of outside clearings would have been less steep. Also, the magnitude of cyclical fluctuations would have been dampened, since consumer and Government expenditures fluctuate cyclically considerably less than many types of business expenditures and in particular of financial transactions giving rise to a considerable volume of checks likely to be exchanged at local clearing houses. The late twenties offer an extreme example of how speculative elements have caused outside (and even more, New York) clearings to increase at a rate considerably exceeding that of the growth of physical output (while prices remained substantially unchanged).

The distinction between the New York and outside data, made at an early date for clearings and continued for debits, appears fully justified by the analysis of the relationship between New York clearings and debits and the volume of financial transactions in New York City, in particular, of payments relating to trading at the New York Stock Exchange. Here again, the deficiency of basic data does not permit more than indirect inference as to the proportion of financial transactions, which might be of the order of 80 to 85 per cent in the case of New York debits. In outside clearings and debits the proportion of financial debits is considerably smaller than in New York. Outside debits are estimated, on the basis of Copeland's work, to exceed the dollar amount of all types of transactions related to the production and distribution of goods and services by about 50 per cent.

The proportion of financial transactions that is included in local clearings and debits data decreases, as a rule, with the size of the community. As debits are used more and more for the purpose of analyzing local rather than national business developments, debits statistics, representing the bulk of local payments for business, personal transactions, and payments by local and State governmental units, still retain their importance as one of the best—and in some cases, the only—continuous monthly series available for the study of fluctuations of business in a given locality. They have the added advantage of being released promptly and of being compiled on a uniform basis, in contrast to local clearings, which reflect also rules and procedures that are not the same for all clearing house associations and that have changed from time to time.

The elimination in 1953 of debits to United States Government and time deposit accounts, suggested in the first edition of this publication, has greatly increased the homogeneity of debits data and their analytical value. The fact that reported debits alone are still roughly twice as large as the value of the final and intermediate purchases of goods and services suggests that the proportion of financial transactions in debits remains high. Since the war, the volume of debits arising from the frequent Treasury refunding and new money operations and the subsequent portfolio adjustments of investors, together with the temporary investment of excess funds by corporations and other holders of large and widely fluctuating balances, has been very considerable. There is some evidence to suggest that efforts to maximize the use of cash balances (accelerated during the period of higher interest rates in the 1954-57 period of economic expansion) have tended to increase the volume of financial debits. In particular, use of repurchase agreements for Government securities, in which an increasing number of nonbanking institutions is participating, gives rise to a large volume of debits in New York City and other financial centers. It is likely that currently debits originating in money market transactions are a much more important share of reported debits than charges to demand deposit accounts arising from stock market activity, which loomed so large in the twenties.

The increasing participation of nonfinancial corporations in the money market complicates any efforts at further "purification" of debits statistics to make them more closely representative of changes in business activity. The accounting records of commercial banks are set up in such a way that individual accounts, or groups of accounts, can be eliminated with relatively small effort, while segregation of certain types of transactions is not practicable. Since current classification of all debits to demand deposit accounts by the nature of the underlying transaction is not feasible, the only way of eliminating the bulk of financial transactions would be to exclude debits to accounts of financial businesses. Agreement on a workable definition of "financial" accounts would not be easy to obtain, but the bulk of financial transactions could probably be removed by eliminating the accounts of members of national stock exchanges, dealers in Government securities, over-the-counter dealers, and investment bankers. Since the number of accounts giving rise exclusively to financial debits is relatively small and their holders are easily identifiable, such a narrowing down of the coverage of debits statistics could be undertaken with a minimum of administrative difficulty.

Such further purification of the debits series might prove to be feasible, but a considerable amount of debits arising from the endeavor of corporations, State treasurers, and other holders of large accounts to invest excess funds for even very short periods would still remain in reported figures, together with a variety of other financial debits which could not be readily eliminated.

As in the past, any future changes in debits statistics are likely to involve a compromise between the endeavor to increase their value for current monetary and business analysis and the desire to preserve the historical comparability that is essential for longer run studies.

The analytical value of debits could be increased by integrating the monthly series with related data that have become available in recent years, such as annual estimates of the ownership of demand deposits. Some suggestions along these lines were made in the first edition of this publication. It was thought that debits could be collected, from a sample of banks, for five depositor categories to match similar categories of nonfinancial accounts covered by the surveys of the ownership of demand deposits conducted annually by the Federal Reserve System. In the meantime, the detail included in these surveys has been reduced, but totals for personal accounts, farm operator accounts, and corporate and noncorporate nonfinancial business would yield four analytically meaningful categories.

Debits to accounts in each of these categories, together with opening (or closing) balances, might be collected from a representative group of banks throughout the country. Rates of turnover for each of these depositor categories would be of great analytical interest. Reporting of debits by the several major groups of non-financial depositors may become feasible if a sufficiently large number of cooperating banks will reclassify their ledgers or maintain the necessary samples. Perhaps the increased mechanization of accounting and other bank operations and the prospective use of electronic equipment will open new possibilities for obtaining significant statistical data on the use of deposit money as a by-product of routine operations.

Bibliography

BOOKS AND PAMPHLETS

Anderson, Benjamin M., *The Value of Money*. New York: Macmillan Co., 1917.

Angell, James W., *The Behavior of Money*. New York: McGraw-Hill Book Co., 1936.

——*Investment and Business Cycles*. New York: McGraw-Hill Book Co., 1941.

Beckhart, Benjamin H., and James G. Smith, *The New York Money Market*, Vol. II. New York: Columbia University Press, 1932.

Boulding, Kenneth E., *Principles of Economic Policy*. Englewood Cliffs: Prentice-Hall, 1958.

Brown, Ernest Henry Phelps, and George L. S. Shackle, *Statistics of Monetary Circulation in England and Wales, 1919-37* (Royal Economic Society Memorandum No. 74). London: 1938.

Burns, Arthur F., and Wesley C. Mitchell, *Measuring Business Cycles*. New York: National Bureau of Economic Research, 1946.

Cannon, James G., *Clearing Houses*. New York: D. Appleton and Co., 1908.

Chandler, Lester V., *The Economics of Money and Banking* (3d ed., rev.). New York: Harper and Bros., 1959.

Chapman, John M., and Ray B. Westerfield, *Branch Banking, Its Historical and Theoretical Position in America and Abroad*. New York: Harper and Bros., 1942.

Clark, Lawrence E., *Central Banking under the Federal Reserve System*. New York: Macmillan Co., 1935.

Copeland, Morris A., *A Study of Money Flows in the United States*. New York: National Bureau of Economic Research, 1952.

Crum, William L., and Alson C. Patton, *An Introduction to Methods of Economic Statistics*. New York: McGraw-Hill Book Co., 1938.

Currie, Lauchlin, *The Supply and Control of Money in the United States* (2d ed., rev.). Cambridge: Harvard University Press, 1935.

Emery, Henry Crosby, *Speculation on the Stock and Produce Exchanges of the United States* (Columbia University Studies in History, Economics and Public Law, No. 18). New York: Longmans, Green and Co., 1896.

Fellner, William, *Monetary Policies and Full Employment* (2d ed.). Berkeley: University of California Press, 1947.

Fisher, Irving, *The Purchasing Power of Money*. New York: Macmillan Co., 1926.

Frickey, Edwin, *Economic Fluctuations in the United States*. Harvard Economic Studies. Cambridge: Harvard University Press, 1942.

Friedman, Milton (ed.), *Studies in the Quantity Theory of Money*. Chicago: University of Chicago Press, 1956.

Friend, Irwin, and Associates, *The Over-the-Counter Securities Markets*. New York: McGraw-Hill Book Co., 1958.

Hansen, Alvin H., *Monetary Theory and Fiscal Policy*. New York: McGraw-Hill Book Co., 1949.

Hart, Albert G., *Defense and the Dollar*. New York: Twentieth Century Fund, 1953.

——*Money, Debt and Economic Activity* (2d ed.). Englewood Cliffs: Prentice-Hall, 1953.

Hegeland, Hugo, *The Quantity Theory of Money. A Critical Study of Its Historical Development and a Restatement*. Göteborg: Elanders Boktryckeri Aktie-bolag, 1951.

Kalecki, Michal, *Studies in Economic Dynamics*. London: George Allen and Unwin, Ltd., 1943.

Kemmerer, Edwin W., *Money and Credit Instruments in Their Relation to General Prices* (2d ed.). New York: Henry Holt, 1909.

Keynes, John Maynard, *Treatise on Money*, Vol. II. New York: Harcourt Brace and Co., 1930.

Kidner, Frank L., *California Business Cycles*. Berkeley: University of California Press, 1946.

Macaulay, Frederick R., *Some Theoretical Problems Suggested by the Movements of Interest Rates, Bond Yields, and Stock Prices in the United States since 1856*. New York: National Bureau of Economic Research, 1938.

Marget, Arthur W., *The Theory of Prices*. Vol. I. New York: Prentice-Hall, 1938.

Meeker, J. Edward, *The Work of the Stock Exchange* (rev. ed.). New York: Ronald Press Co., 1930.

Mitchell, Wesley C., *Business Cycles*. Berkeley: University of California Press, 1913.

——*Business Cycles: The Problem and Its Setting*. New York: National Bureau of Economic Research, 1927.

——*What Happens during Business Cycles* (Studies in Business Cycles No. 5). New York: National Bureau of Economic Research, 1951.

Neff, Philip, and Annette Weifenbach, *Business Cycles in Selected Industrial Areas*. Haynes Foundation. Berkeley: University of California Press, 1949.

Neisser, Hans, "Umlaufsgeschwindigkeit der Bankdepositen," in *Handwörter-buch des Bankwesens*. Berlin: 1933.

Norton, John Pease, *Statistical Studies in the New York Money Market Preceded by a Brief Analysis under the Theory of Money and Credit*. New York: Macmillan Co., 1902.

Pigou, Arthur C., *Industrial Fluctuations* (2d ed.). London: Macmillan, 1930.

Schumpeter, Joseph A., *Business Cycles*, Vols. I-II (1st ed.). New York: McGraw-Hill Book Co., 1939.

DEBITS AND CLEARINGS

Silberling, Norman J., *Dynamics of Business*. New York: McGraw-Hill Book Co., 1943.

Snyder, Carl, *Business Cycles and Business Measurements*. New York: Macmillan Co., 1927.

Spahr, Walter E., *The Clearing and Collection of Checks*. New York: Bankers Publishing Co., 1926.

Thomas, Rollin G., *Our Modern Banking and Monetary System* (3d ed.). Englewood Cliffs: Prentice-Hall, 1957.

Thralls, Jerome, *The Clearing House*. New York: American Bankers Association, 1916.

Westerfield, Ray B., *Money, Credit and Banking* (rev. ed.). New York: Ronald Press Co., 1947.

Willis, Henry Parker, *The Theory and Practice of Central Banking, with Special Reference to American Experience, 1913-1935*. New York: Harper and Bros., 1936.

ARTICLES

Bailey, Dudley P., "The Clearing House System," *The Bankers Magazine*, February-June 1890, pp. 606-11, 660-69, 751-63, 845-52, and 917-18.

Behrman, J. N., "The Short-Term Interest Rate and the Velocity of Circulation," *Econometrica*, April 1948, pp. 185-90.

Burgess, W. Randolph, "Velocity of Bank Deposits," *Journal of the American Statistical Association*, June 1923, p. 728.

Burns, Arthur F., "The Quantity Theory and Price Stabilization," *American Economic Review*, December 1929, pp. 561-79.

——"The Relative Importance of Check and Cash Payments," *Journal of the American Statistical Association*, December 1929, pp. 420-24.

Copeland, Morris A., "An Estimate of Total Volume of Debits to Individual Accounts in the United States," *Journal of the American Statistical Association*, September 1928, pp. 301-03.

——"Money, Trade, and Prices—A Test of Causal Primacy," *Quarterly Journal of Economics*, August 1929, pp. 648-66.

——"Special Purpose Indexes for the Equation of Exchange for the United States, 1919-1927," *Journal of the American Statistical Association*, June 1929, pp. 109-22.

——"Tracing Money Flows through the United States Economy," *American Economic Review, Proceedings*, May 1947, pp. 31-49.

Crum, William L., "Revision of the Index of General Business Conditions," *Review of Economic Statistics*, November 1928, pp. 202-12.

——"Weekly Fluctuations in Outside Bank Debits," *Review of Economic Statistics*, January 1927, pp. 30-36.

des Essars, Pierre, "La Vitesse de la circulation de la monnaie," *Journal de la Societé de Statistique de Paris*, April 1895, p. 149.

Eckler, A. Ross, "A Measure of the Severity of Depressions, 1873-1932," *Review of Economic Statistics*, May 1933, pp. 75-81.

Frickey, Edwin, "Bank Clearings Outside New York City, 1875-1914," *Review of Economic Statistics*, October 1925, pp. 252-62.

——"Outside Bank Debits Corrected for Seasonal Variation: Monthly and Weekly, 1919-31," *Review of Economic Statistics*, May 1931, pp. 76-84.

——"Revision of the Index of General Business Conditions," *Review of Economic Statistics*, May 1932, pp. 80-87.

——"A Statistical Study of Bank Clearings, 1875-1914," *Review of Economic Statistics*, May 1930, pp. 90-99 and August 1930, pp. 112-38.

Garvy, George, "Rivals and Interlopers in the History of the New York Security Market," *Journal of Political Economy*, June 1944, pp. 128-43.

——"Velocity of Time Deposits," *Journal of the American Statistical Association*, June 1953, pp. 176-91.

——"Structural Aspects of Money Velocity," *Quarterly Journal of Economics*, June 1959, pp. 74-96.

Kalecki, Michal, "The Short-Term Rate of Interest and the Velocity of Cash Circulation," *Review of Economic Statistics*, May 1941, pp. 97-99.

King, Willford I., "Recent Monetary Experiments and their Effect upon the Theory of Money and Prices," *Journal of the American Statistical Association*, June 1935, pp. 387-400.

Matthews, Ada M., "New York Bank Clearings and Stock Prices, 1866-1914," *Review of Economic Statistics*, October 1926, pp. 184-98.

Matthews, Ada M., and A. Ross Eckler, "Regional Business Conditions: A Study of Bank Debits," *Review of Economic Statistics*, August 1928, pp. 140-55.

Mitchell, George W., "Exploring Changes in Money Use," *Memoria*, V Reunión de Técnicos de los Bancos Centrales del Continente Americano, pp. 251-69. Bogotá: Banco de la República, 1957.

Neff, Philip, "Interregional Cyclical Differentials; Causes, Measurement and Significance," *American Economic Review, Proceedings*, May 1949, pp. 105-19.

Persons, Warren M., "Quantity Theory as Tested by Kemmerer," *Quarterly Journal of Economics*, February 1908.

——"An Index of General Business Conditions," *Review of Economic Statistics*, April 1919, pp. 111-51.

——"The Revised Index of General Business Conditions," *Review of Economic Statistics*, July 1923, pp. 187-95.

Persons, Warren M., William L. Crum, and Edwin Frickey, "Revision of the Index of General Business Conditions," *Review of Economic Statistics*, April 1926, pp. 64-68.

Ritter, Lawrence S., "Income Velocity and Anti-Inflationary Monetary Policy," *American Economic Review*, March 1959, pp. 120-29.

Rogers, James H., "The Effect of Stock Speculation on the New York Money Market," *Quarterly Journal of Economics*, May 1926, p. 437.

Seibert, Joseph C., "Bank Debits as a Market Indicator," *Miami Business Review*, January 1949. The School of Business Administration, Miami University, Oxford, Ohio.

Silberling, Norman J., "The Mystery of Clearings," *The Annalist*, August 14, 1916, pp. 198 and 223.

Snyder, Carl, "Deposit Activity as a Measure of Business Activity," *Review of Economic Statistics*, October 1924, pp. 253-57.

——"A New Index of Business Activity," *Journal of the American Statistical Association*, March 1924, pp. 36-41.

——"A New Clearings Index of Business for Fifty Years," *Journal of the American Statistical Association*, September 1924, pp. 329-35.

——"A New Index of the General Price Level from 1875," *Journal of the American Statistical Association*, June 1924, p. 190.

——"A New Index of the Volume of Trade," *Journal of the American Statistical Association*, December 1923, pp. 949-63.

——"Industrial Growth and Monetary Theory," *Economic Forum*, Summer 1933, pp. 275-90.

——"New Measures in the Equation of Exchange," *American Economic Review*, December 1924, pp. 699-713.

——"New Measures of the Relations of Credit and Trade," *Proceedings of the Academy of Political Science*, January 1930, pp. 16-34.

——"The Problem of Monetary and Economic Stability," *Quarterly Journal of Economics*, February 1935, pp. 173-205.

Tobin, James, "Liquidity Preference and Monetary Policy," *Review of Economic Statistics*, May 1947, pp. 124-31.

Vining, Rutledge, "Regional Variation in Cyclical Fluctuations Viewed as a Frequency Distribution," *Econometrica*, July 1945, pp. 183-219.

——"The Region as an Economic Entity and Certain Variations to be Observed in the Study of Systems of Regions," *American Economic Review, Proceedings*, May 1949, pp. 89-104.

Warburton, Clark, "Money Velocity and Monetary Policy," *Review of Economic Statistics*, November 1948, pp. 304-14.

——"Monetary Velocity and the Rate of Interest," *Review of Economics and Statistics*, August 1950, pp. 256-57.

——"Quantity and Frequency of Use of Money in the United States, 1919-45," *Journal of Political Economy*, October 1946, pp. 436-50.

——"The Secular Trend in Monetary Velocity," *Quarterly Journal of Economics*, February 1949, pp. 68-91.

——"The Volume of Money and the Price Level between the World Wars," *Journal of Political Economy*, June 1945, pp. 150-63.

Working, Holbrook, "Prices and the Quantity of Circulating Medium, 1890-1921," *Quarterly Journal of Economics*, February 1923, pp. 228-56.

FEDERAL RESERVE SYSTEM PUBLICATIONS

Board of Governors of the Federal Reserve System.
——*Banking and Monetary Statistics.* Washington: 1943.
——*Federal Reserve Bulletin.*
  ——"The Monetary System of the United States," February 1953, pp. 98-109.
  ——"Revision of Monthly Bank Debits and Weekly Reporting Member Bank Series," April 1953, pp. 355-57.
——*Flow of Funds in the United States, 1939-1953.* Washington: 1955.
——Garvy, George, *The Development of Bank Debits and Clearings and their Use in Economic Analysis* (1st ed. of present volume). Washington: 1952.

Federal Reserve Bank of Atlanta. *Monthly Review.*
——Brandt, Harry, "The Turnover of Money," September 1957, pp. 3-4.
——Taylor, Charles T., "Bank Debits Rise Reflects Business Expansion," June 1955, p. 6.
  ——"Deposit Growth in Georgia Member Banks," June 1950, pp. 56-57.
  ——"Deposit Turnover: A Guide to Sixth District Economic Activity," August 1948, pp. 86-87.
  ——"Sixth District Bank Debits," June 1946, pp. 62-63.
——Young, Robert M., "A Barometer of Sixth District Spending: New Indexes of Bank Debits," October 1958, pp. 4-5.

Federal Reserve Bank of Boston. *New England Business Review.*
——"The Turnover Rate of Money," February 1959.

Federal Reserve Bank of Chicago. *Business Conditions.*
——"Another Look at the Money Supply," March 1958, pp. 12-16.
——"Savings Levels and Turnover," May 1951, pp. 6-8.
——"Harder Working Dollars," September 1956, pp. 5-7.
——"Checkbook Spending—a Yardstick for Measuring Area Activity," February 1955, pp. 5-9.
——"Turnover of Midwest Savings Deposits," March 1954, pp. 15-16.
——"More Business—More Checks," May 1953, p. 16.
——"Money Supply and Money Turnover," May 1951, pp. 6-8.

Federal Reserve Bank of Cleveland.
——*Business Trends.*
  ——Jones, O. H., "Bank Debits as Economic Indicators," February 4, 1956.
  ——Wert, J. E., "Bank Debits and Local Business Trends," September 28, 1958.
——*Monthly Business Review.*
  ——"Bank Debits as a Local Business Indicator," November 1957, pp. 2-6.
  ——"Local Trends in Volume of Bank Debits," August 1954, pp. 9-11.

DEBITS AND CLEARINGS

Federal Reserve Bank of Dallas. *Monthly Business Review.*
——"Bank Debits, End-of-Month Deposits, and Annual Rate of Turnover of Deposits in 24 Reporting Cities, Eleventh Federal Reserve District," *Supplement*, August 1, 1947.

Federal Reserve Bank of Minneapolis. *Monthly Review.*
——"Bank Debits—A Measure of Spending," June 1957, p. 7.
——"Bank Debits Show Growth for Most District Cities," December 1955, p. 4.

Federal Reserve Bank of New York. *Monthly Review.*
——"The Velocity of Demand Deposits in New York City," August 1954, pp. 112-15.
——"Bank Debits and Velocity: Economic Indicators," May 1953, pp. 75-77.
——"Postwar Changes in the Velocity of Deposits," March 1949, pp. 27-29.

Federal Reserve Bank of Richmond. *Monthly Review.*
——"Monetary Velocity—How Active a Partner?" April 1957, pp. 3-4.

Federal Reserve Bank of St. Louis. *Monthly Review.*
——"Bank Debits and Economic Activity," November 1956, pp. 125-33.

———————